WITHDRAWN

Teach Them Diligently
The Personal Story of a Community Rabbi

MAGGID

Berel Wein

TEACH THEM DILIGENTLY ושננתם לבניך

THE PERSONAL STORY OF A COMMUNITY RABBI

Maggid Books

Teach Them Diligently:
The Personal Story of a Community Rabbi

First Edition, 2014

Maggid Books
An imprint of Koren Publishers Jerusalem Ltd.

POB 8531, New Milford, CT 06776-8531, USA
& POB 4044, Jerusalem 91040, Israel
www.korenpub.com

© Berel Wein 2014

Cover Photo (Portrait) © Yonit Schiller

Cover Photo (Background) © Ida Crown Jewish Academy

The publication of this book was made possible
through the generous support of *Torah Education in Israel.*

ISBN 978 159 264 348 6, *hardcover*

A CIP catalogue record for this title is
available from the British Library

Printed and bound in the United States

Dedicated to the family of my life,
all of our generations of Weins,
Levins, Lipschutzes, Kellers, Teitelbaums, Gettingers,
Gewirtzes, Cohens, Silberbergs, Schochets and Torgows
in love, affection, and great pride

Contents

Introduction

I have always considered autobiographical works somewhat presumptuous. Why should anyone be interested in the details of someone else's life? Naturally, that observation applies to *others'* autobiographies. But sharing *my* life's experiences with complete strangers is different, for they'll surely value my story.

I've toyed with writing my autobiography for years. The Talmud teaches us that Moshe, Yehoshua, and Shmuel, among others, each wrote "his book." There is a different quality to one's own book. It is more poignant, personal, and accurate than books written by others about a person's life. Lately, I spend much time and effort reviewing the decades that have passed, assessing my actions, accomplishments, and failures. My grown grandchildren have urged me to record my life experiences for them, for I am their connection to their illustrious ancestors and to a world that I at least glimpsed, but that is no more and never will be again.

Rabbi Yehuda HaNasi, the remarkable and holy editor of the Mishnah, attributed his greatness in Torah and piety to the fact that he once saw Rabbi Meir's back. He stated that had he seen him face to face, he would have been even greater. Well, I was privileged to see Eastern European Jewry's "back," through my family and teachers, and I feel compelled to share those experiences with my descendants. They've asked me about my parents and grandparents, my teachers, and the distinguished people I've been honored to meet and know, the events private and national that helped shape my outlook, and the twists and turns of life. I have recounted many impressions and vignettes to my grandchildren, but they insist they want it all in writing. How does one refuse a grandchild?

So here it is.

This is not a tell-all book, not about me nor about others. Yet I hope it is an honest assessment not only of my years and experiences, but of Jewish history in the second half of the twentieth century and the first decade of the twenty-first. Naturally, it is oriented to Jewish life and thought – after all, I am a rabbi – but it also covers my reactions to world events that have transpired in my lifetime. One can no longer live (if ever he could) in a cocoon, shutting out the world beyond. We are all influenced – physically, emotionally, intellectually, and even spiritually – by events taking place outside our narrow society.

I have not condemned anyone in this book, though as a lawyer – and later, for most of my life, as a rabbi – I often found myself in contentious situations between people who turned against me. I have always attempted to be a peaceful person, and I'm no zealot. I try to judge people charitably and steer clear of unnecessary controversy. Nevertheless, many times I've been deeply hurt by others' actions. But that is life, and no one passes through it unscathed. I harbor no grudges against anyone, and I can truly say that somehow, in the long run, I've emerged from all these incidents stronger and more confident.

The passage of time and the broader perspective that life grants us allows people to arrive at serenity and inner peace. So it is for me, and so, I imagine, will it be for those who come after me. Too bad we don't know at thirty what we've learned about people and life by the time we've reached seventy-five-plus.

The rabbis tell us that Moshe Rabbeinu wrote the last few lines of the Torah "in tears." There are many interpretations of this moving aggadic metaphor. But what is obvious is that at the end of his life Moshe wrote with deep emotion. In that sense, this book is also written "in tears." Many of the most important people in my life are no longer alive, and they have left a void in my heart that is not easily filled. Many "should have's" and "could have's" have reared their ugly heads while writing this book. But on the whole, my "tears" are ones of happiness, satisfaction, and gratitude. I consider myself privileged to have lived in this era, of great and awesome events. I was fortunate that my parents immigrated to the United States, sparing me the fate of my many cousins in Eastern Europe during World War II. I also lived during a good time in the United States, benefiting from a decline of anti-Semitism and a new openness in American life. I saw the injustices done to people of color in America begin to be corrected by legislation and societal behavior. I was privileged to witness and participate in the renaissance of Orthodox Jewish life in America and Israel. I experienced the realization of the age-old Jewish dream with the establishment and continued growth of the State of Israel and its ingathering of the exiles. I have been able to live my latter years in the holy city of Jerusalem, and even to serve as the rabbi of a prestigious congregation there. And I have been privileged to see the fourth generation of my immediate family. My cup truly "runneth over," and my gratitude to the Lord is genuine, though undoubtedly inadequate. So my "tears" are not those of sadness, but those of serenity and appreciation.

Finally I am indebted to the many people over the years who have helped me in so many ways. I will specify many of them in this book. My congregants in Chicago, Miami Beach, Monsey, and Jerusalem are worthy of special appreciation, as are my rabbinic colleagues in those communities and throughout the Jewish world. My publishers, devoted secretaries, and office and administrative staff have always been kind, loyal, and most helpful to me. This is especially true of Elaine Gilbert and the Cubac family, the mainstays of my Destiny Foundation's offices in Monsey, and Jerusalem, respectively. My longtime editor, Charlotte Friedland, has whipped my meandering prose into readable shape, and I am most grateful for her efforts and talents. I also wish to thank Gila Fine, Tomi Mager, and Suzanne Libenson of Maggid Books for their excellent editorial and proofreading work. Their patience and skill in dealing with my sometimes convoluted writing style is to be commended and is most appreciated. Needless to say, my wife Mira has helped me rebuild my life and graces our home with charm, good taste, and the warmth of caring love. My children, grandchildren, and great-grandchildren are naturally my pride and joy. May the Lord bless them all.

Berel Wein
Jerusalem
Winter 5774/2014

Chapter 1

Early Influences

"How are you going to help rebuild the Jewish People?"

One of my most vivid childhood memories is of my father taking me with him to Chicago's Midway Airport to greet Rabbi Isaac Halevi Herzog, the chief rabbi of Palestine after the Second World War. Almost all the distinguished Orthodox rabbis in Chicago came to the airport that day to welcome him. I remember him alighting from the plane and walking down the stairs in his shiny top hat, holding his cane in one hand and a Tanach (Bible) in the other. With his silver beard and aristocratic demeanor, he was a majestic presence.

We all accompanied Rabbi Herzog to the yeshiva, where he delivered a forty-five-minute Talmudic lecture in Yiddish. I still remember his topic, and though I was not yet *bar mitzvah*, I pretty much followed his discourse. After that, he addressed us in English. Having been a rabbi in Dublin, he spoke with a slight Irish brogue, which I found somewhat incongruous with his Eastern European rabbinical appearance.

Rabbi Herzog told us he had been to the Vatican and had asked Pope Pius XII to return the thousands of Jewish children entrusted to Catholic institutions in Europe by parents hoping to save them from annihilation at the hands of the Germans. The pope had flatly refused, claiming that since all the children had been baptized upon entering those institutions, they could not now be given over to those who would raise them in a different faith. Overcome with emotion, the rabbi put his head down on the lectern and wept bitterly. We were all in shock, as the enormity of the Jewish tragedy of World War II began sinking in.

Then Rabbi Herzog defiantly raised his head and looked at the young men gathered before him. "I cannot save those thousands of Jewish children," he declared, "but I ask of you – how are you going to help rebuild the Jewish People?" Afterward, when we filed by him to shake his hand and receive his blessing, he repeated to each and every one of us: "Did you understand what I said to you? Don't forget it."

All my life, Rabbi Herzog's words have echoed in my ears and soul. Numerous times in my rabbinic career, I've been discouraged and downhearted. But then I remembered his words. They have continually inspired and challenged me, shaping many of my decisions and actions.

To put those decisions and actions into context, we must go back to the beginning. I was born in Chicago on 9 Nisan 5694/March 25, 1934. I was named after my paternal grandfather, Dov Berel, who had just passed away at a relatively young age as life spans go in the Wein family. And yes, my name – Berel Wein – was the butt of many jokes during my school years. My parents refused to anglicize the name or allow me a more American alternative. I sometimes resented that, but ultimately my name became a source of pride.

As an only son, I was an adult from the moment I was born. My father, Rabbi Zev Wein, was a distinguished rabbi in Chicago, and my mother, Esther Rubinstein Wein, was the daughter of Rabbi Chaim Zvi Rubinstein, also a leading congregational rabbi in Chicago, the founder and one of the *roshei yeshiva* (deans) of Beis Medrash L'Torah/Hebrew Theological College (then of Chicago, and currently in Skokie, Illinois). My mother was an accomplished teacher and very formidable, both intellectually and personally.

The Wein family was from the small Lithuanian village of Ratzki, near the Prussian border. They had lived there for generations, serving as renowned rabbis and lay leaders. My aunt Shoshana Freed once told me we were descended from Spanish exiles who eventually got to Lithuania,

Right to left: Me, my father, and my son Chaim Zvi

and the name Wein originated from a stopover in Vienna. Apparently, such renaming was not uncommon. Rabbi Baruch Halevi Epstein, author of *Torah Temimah*, relates that his original family name was Benevisti and that his ancestors also traveled from Spain to Lithuania, stopping in the German city of Ebstein. He states that every Epstein who's a Levi is really a Benevisti, a descendant of Spanish Jewish exiles.

At any rate, my father left Ratzki to attend the Slabodka Yeshiva (also in Lithuania) for one year and then transferred to Yeshiva Shaar Hatorah in Grodno, Poland/Lithuania, headed by the legendary Rabbi Shimon HaKohen Shkop. My father often told me that whenever he imagined the high priest of Israel, he pictured Rabbi Shkop.

Immediately after World War I, Shaar Hatorah lacked a full set of the Babylonian Talmud. In fact, in all of Grodno only one complete set had survived the war (and later pogroms), and its very rich owner kept it under lock and key. So Rabbi Shkop set out to create a "living Talmud" in his yeshiva. He sent students to the man's home to memorize the tractates missing from the yeshiva's own library. My father was one of those students. He committed to memory tractate Chullin as well as several others. Gifted with a prodigious memory and great diligence in his Torah studies, my father could later recall entire tractates by heart, even when he was over ninety years old.

In 1925, he went to Palestine, joining his brother Dovid in the Slabodka Yeshiva in Jerusalem. When the yeshiva moved to Hebron, he stayed in Jerusalem to attend the Mercaz HaRav yeshiva, established by Rabbi Avraham Yitzchak Kook. The yeshiva's teachers were noted scholars, and its students were known for their superior Torah knowledge. Because of my father's outstanding memory and familiarity with a wide array of rabbinic works, Rabbi Kook dubbed him "my bookcase." Father was greatly influenced by Rabbi Kook's holy personality. He told me that hearing Rabbi Kook speak at the Seudah Shlishit in the yeshiva transported one "almost to *Gan Eden*" – the World to Come. He was not alone in his opinion. Scholars from all segments of Jerusalem's perpetually fractured religious community came together regularly to enjoy this Shabbat experience as well.

While my father was in Jerusalem, Rabbi Kook and Rabbis Issur Zalman Meltzer, Yaakov Charlop, Shmuel Rapaport, Moshe Mordechai Epstein, and Abba Yaakov Borochov all granted him *semichah* (rabbinic ordination).

Class photo of Mercaz Harav yeshiva, 1928
(my father, top row, center, second from right)

In 1929, Rabbi Shimon Shkop left Lithuania and came to New York to teach Talmud at the Rabbi Isaac Elchanan Theological Seminary (now part of Yeshiva University).[1] Rabbi Shimon influenced my father to come to New York in order to help build a stronger foundation of Torah knowledge within the student body of the yeshiva. During that time, my father had a patron, Rabbi Aaron Charney of Bayonne, New Jersey. His wife was a distant relative of my father's and also born and raised in Ratzki. My father spent Shabbat and holidays with the Charneys. I met Rabbi Charney a number of times, finding him to be the absolute prototype of the traditional Lithuanian rabbi. He was a fine orator, an author of rabbinic works, and a most engaging and enlightened personality. (I have known his wonderful family for several generations now, and I treasure our relationship.) My father's other great patron was Rabbi Dr. Bernard Revel, the head of the yeshiva. Father later received *semichah* from him, Rabbi Shkop, and Rabbis Moshe Soloveitchik and Moshe Zev Margolies.

My father arrived in New York on the same boat as Rabbi Dr. Shmuel Belkin. They had something else in common as well. There was a prize of $500 for outstanding Torah scholarship in the yeshiva, established by Israel Rokeach (of the Rokeach Food Corporation). Both my father and Rabbi Belkin received this prize in 1929. (They remained fast friends for decades.)

Dr. Revel knew my future grandfather, Rabbi Rubinstein, in Chicago, and he knew he had unmarried daughters. Now that my father had won the Rokeach prize – equivalent to a year's salary – Dr. Revel suggested that he go to Chicago and meet the daughters.

That's how my parents met, marrying in 1932. My grandfather arranged for my father to become the rabbi of the Anshei Odessa synagogue on Chicago's Jewish West Side. I was born in 1934, and in 1939 my father became the rabbi of the much larger Beis Medrash Hagadol

---

1. Rabbi Shimon told my father that "European Jewry was all played out" and that the future of the Jewish People lay only in America and in the Land of Israel. Yet Rabbi Shkop himself later acceded to the request of the Chofetz Chaim (Rabbi Yisrael Meir Kagan) and Rabbi Chaim Ozer Grodzensky and returned to Lithuania to head the yeshiva in Grodno. He left New York with a heavy heart, sensing perhaps that he could have had a greater impact on Jewish life by staying put.

My parents at their 35th wedding anniversary

Bnei Yaakov Anshei Luknik synagogue, a most prestigious position. The synagogue moved a number of times and added the name Kesser Maariv, but my father remained its rabbi.[2]

Father had one sister and four brothers. After studying in yeshiva, Eliezer, his oldest brother, was caught up in the zeitgeist and became a Labor Zionist activist. He moved to the Land of Israel in 1921, paving the streets of Tel Aviv with his bare hands, despite his degrees in education. He later became an expert on bees and the production of honey, serving as a consultant to many honey producers, Jews and Arabs alike. Eliezer married late and lived in Hadera. He swam every morning in the Mediterranean, even in his nineties. In his last decade, he returned to Jewish observance.

The second brother was Rabbi Dovid Wein, a student in the Slabodka Yeshiva. He arrived in the Land of Israel in 1923 with a contingent from the yeshiva, then headed by the *Alter* of Slabodka, Rabbi Nosson Zvi Finkel. The yeshiva was established in Jerusalem, but the young men of Slabodka, with their European dress and relatively worldly

---

2. He served as a rabbi in Chicago for over fifty years, retiring only when he came to live with my family in Monsey, New York, in the 1980s.

outlook, were derided by Jerusalem zealots, and Rabbi Finkel prudently moved the yeshiva to Hebron to avoid friction. Sadly, the yeshiva suffered in the deadly 1929 pogrom at the hands of a rioting Arab mob. Uncle Dovid, who survived the pogrom, married and moved to Holon, where he served for a while as a community security guard. He was a great scholar, a clever leader, and a person of nobility, piety, and holiness. Every Elul, he would return to the Slabodka Yeshiva (now back in Jerusalem and renamed the Hebron Yeshiva) to gain spiritual strength for the upcoming Days of Awe. In the 1930s, he became the rabbi of the main synagogue in Holon, serving in that post until his death in 1967. He and his wife, Aunt Rishel (Miletsky), never had children.

My father was the third son in the family. After him came Rabbi Aharon Yehuda Wein. Aharon Yehuda studied in Slabodka and Radin, becoming a formidable scholar and the rabbi of Vidz, a town in Lithuania famed for its outstanding rabbinic leaders over the ages. The Ponivezher Rav, Rabbi Yosef Shlomo Kahaneman, was once rabbi in Vidz, and told me how wonderful Jewish life there had been.

Aharon Yehuda's father-in-law had himself served as rabbi of the town until moving to South Africa. Remaining in Vidz proved tragic for Aharon Yehuda. When the Russians occupied Lithuania in 1940, their murderous commissars (many of them Jewish) killed him and his whole family for being "counter-revolutionaries." He had refused to cooperate with the Russians in destroying local Jewish life. I clearly remember the terrible day that Rabbi Ephraim Oshry,[3] himself a survivor of the horrors of World War II, arrived at our home in Chicago and told my father the awful news. Though I was only eleven, the story made the Holocaust real and personal to me. At that very early age I also became a confirmed anti-Communist. I couldn't conceive of any cause or ideology worthy of the murder of my uncle, aunt, and little cousins.

World War II was a fact of my childhood. I remember hearing on our radio Adolf Hitler's screeching rants and the roar of the crowd listening to him, while my parents paled and wept. I remember the date "which will live in infamy," December 7, 1941, as I returned with my mother

---

3. Author of *The Annihilation of Lithuanian Jewry* (New York: Judaica Press, 1995).

from a movie theater to hear the news that the Japanese had attacked Pearl Harbor. America was at war. I didn't know what that would mean.

I don't recall the war causing me any inconvenience, aside from having to sing patriotic songs at school. But I understood from the adults around me that something terrible was happening to the Jewish People in Europe. I was also greatly concerned about the Jews in the Land of Israel, and childishly dreamed about helping fight the Arabs, the British, and the Germans there.

Food was rationed during the war, but I don't remember our family ever lacking basic necessities. My father's congregants brought us food to help feed our constant guests. As there were no home freezers then, my mother was always cooking. The war became less remote when the son of my grandfather's neighbor lost his life fighting in the Pacific. We shared the family's anguish. Only later did I learn that very close relatives of mine were also killed in the war.

The youngest of my father's brothers was Rabbi Tuvia Wein. He studied in the legendary Chofetz Chaim's yeshiva in Radin in the early 1930s. When my grandfather Berel died suddenly on a visit to Warsaw (sadly, I could not locate his grave in the Jewish cemetery there), my grandmother Esther Chana (Romberg) Wein (a direct descendant of the Vilna Gaon) left the town of Ratzki with her children, my Uncle Tuvia and Aunt Shoshana, and immigrated to the Land of Israel. The former joined Poalei Agudas Yisrael and worked as a laborer before becoming an outstanding teacher in the *Charedi* school system in Ramle and Rechovot. Uncle Tuvia was famed throughout religious Israel as a miniature Chofetz Chaim because of his guarded tongue, Torah scholarship, and piety. He authored *Yayn Hatov,* a series of seminal works on the Targum (the Aramaic exposition of the Bible), and in many respects was the mainstay of the Rechovot religious community.

Uncle Tuviah married Aunt Sarah, and their two daughters, Batya Kurlansky and Shulamit Ginsberg, and their extended families are still very close to our family. Any visit to their home, no matter what time of day or night, included a full meat meal; no excuse, rational explanation, or argument could ever change that custom. Aunt Sarah would command, "Eat!" and you ate. Whenever I visited them in Rechovot, Aunt Sarah would run downstairs and invite the taxi driver up to have a bite too. Most of those tough Israelis couldn't escape without eating something in her home. My wife once complimented Aunt Sarah on her strudel. From that day on, we always received strudel from her through Israeli visitors to America, and later through guests in our home in Jerusalem. Uncle Tuvia and Aunt Sarah were the kindest, gentlest souls imaginable, and their love for people – all people – and for the Land of Israel was palpable. Visiting them was always a spiritual experience.

My grandmother ultimately lived with her daughter Shoshana in south Tel Aviv, close to the Jaffa border. Aunt Shoshana was a most wondrous person. She was extremely clever, knowledgeable, and industrious, with a great sense of humor. She married Chaim Freed, and they had five children.[4] Born in Vilna, Uncle Chaim was a Torah scholar, but he worked as a toolmaker/mechanic. His workshop provided small arms for the Haganah in the struggle against the British and the Arabs. Aunt Shoshana was the executive secretary of Ponivezh Yeshiva. The Ponivezher Rav told me that "she *was* the yeshiva." I remember once calling her there to say hello on one of my trips to Israel, and she quickly told me that since the yeshiva was paying her salary, she couldn't talk to me at work, and I should call her at home that night. Those Jews of Ratzki were truly special. They were modest, humble, serene, optimistic, and very perceptive about life and people. They had minimal physical expectations from life and great discipline in behavior, speech, and attitude. They represented the best qualities of Lithuanian Jewry. I always felt humbled in their presence.

My mother's family, the Rubinsteins, came from Buten, a small village near Belarus. The original family name wasn't Rubinstein, but my grandfather took it on to avoid grueling, long-term service in the Russian army. If a family had only one son, he was exempted from military duty; thus, by having different last names, everyone in the family could claim he was an only son. This tactic was common in Russia during the czarist anti-Jewish campaigns of the nineteenth century.

---

4. The oldest, my cousin Nechama, is married to the well-known holy *mashgiach* Rabbi Dan Segal.

In 1884, when my grandfather, Chaim Zvi, was fourteen, he arrived at the famed Etz Chaim Yeshiva in Volozhin, Lithuania/ Belarus. He became a devoted disciple of Rabbi Naftali Zvi Yehuda Berlin (the "Netziv"), the head of the yeshiva, and also studied under his associate, the famed Rabbi Chaim Soloveitchik. My grandfather received *semichah* from both of these Torah greats. He once described to me the intensity and the enormous amounts of text studied in the yeshiva, and doubted that such a standard would ever be seen again. One winter semester, from Succot to Pesach, he himself completed studying two difficult Talmudic tractates – Gittin and Kiddushin – in depth and with many commentaries. This in addition to preparing for the daily Talmud lectures. In 1892, the yeshiva was closed by the czarist government with the aid – and probably at the instigation – of the Jewish "*maskilim*" ("enlightened ones"). Rabbi Berlin left Russia for Jerusalem. He took with him a number of devoted students who begged to accompany him, among them my grandfather, who was not yet married.

The group moved on to Warsaw, aiming to reach Turkey and then Palestine. However, Rabbi Berlin suffered a debilitating stroke and died a few months later. On my only visit to Poland, in the 1990s, I visited his grave – Rabbi Chaim Soloveitchik is buried next to him – in the War- saw Jewish cemetery.

My grandfather then married Chaya Sarah Rabinowitz, a young widow with an infant son. (That son was later studying at a yeshiva in Galicia when World War I caught up with him, and he became a victim of its horrors.) Chaya Sarah was a niece of the famed Hasidic master Rabbi Zadok HaKohen Rabinowitz of Pshischa (and later Lublin). Reb Zadok was the only Hasid in the family.

My grandparents continued on to the Land of Israel, settling in Jaffa, where the famed Rabbi Avraham Yitzchak Kook became the rabbi in 1904. He and my grandfather had been friends as students in Volozhin. Rabbi Rubinstein founded a yeshiva called Shaarei Torah, whose building remains a Jaffa landmark. The family eventually moved to Jerusalem, where he served on the rabbinic court headed by Rabbi Shmuel Salant.

In 1911, my grandfather was sent to America to raise funds for Jerusalem charities. In Chicago he encountered immigration difficulties and was threatened with jail and/or deportation. Lacking a rabbi, the Jewish community of South Chicago offered to help him if he stayed on. This story is reminiscent of the famous "Four Captives" of Babylonia who were ransomed by Jewish communities in Italy, Morocco, and Spain provided that they remain as rabbis in those communities. Never underestimate the powers and tactics of Jews in hiring – or firing – a rabbi.

In any event, my grandfather agreed, bringing over the family from Jerusalem, and that is how I came to be born in Chicago.

My Rubinstein grandparents had six children. The boys were Naftali, Zadok, and Shmuel. The girls were Judith, Esther (my mother), and Rachel.

Naftali was a *shochet*/rabbi/teacher in Aurora, Illinois, near Chicago. His daughter, Bertha Merzon, was my first cousin, and her grandson is my beloved relative Gary Torgow, a lay leader of American Orthodoxy.

Zadok was a rabbi in Milwaukee and later in Ventura, California, while Shmuel worked as a car dealer in Chicago.

Rachel married Rabbi Jacob Schochet, a student from the Slabodka Yeshiva and a Hebrew teacher in Chicago. Their only child, my closest cousin, Rabbi Elijah Judah Schochet, was a rabbi in Los Angeles for forty years until his retirement. We are the same age and were classmates in elementary school until the Schochets left for California in 1947. Our families are still close. The Schochets are related to the late, great Rabbi Yaakov Kamenetsky and his descendants.

Judith married Moshe Silverman, another former Slabodka student and a teacher in Chicago's Marks Nathan Jewish Orphan Home. After my grandfather was widowed in 1935, the Silvermans moved in with him (at 3315 Douglas Boulevard) until they left for Los Angeles in 1950.

Very few of my peers had living grandparents. My mother's father was the only grandparent I knew: As noted, my paternal grandfather passed away before I was born (and I am named after him); my maternal grandmother died while I was still an infant; and my paternal grandmother lived in Tel Aviv, so I never saw her.

In 1919, Grandfather Rubinstein founded Beis Medrash L'Torah/ Hebrew Theological College with three students, who learned and lived in his home. The yeshiva was incorporated in 1921, with Rabbi Saul Silber as president and Rabbi Nissan Yablonsky, a famed Slabodka Torah scholar, as *rosh yeshiva*. My grandfather taught the second-highest level.

R. Chaim Zvi Halevi Rubinstein

I knew Grandfather from my infancy until his death, when I was ten. I studied Torah with him, joined in his Pesach *Sedarim*, and sat on his lap on Simchat Torah afternoon, when his students came to his home to sing and eat and discuss Torah. He brought me into the yeshiva's late afternoon class at age nine to begin intensive study. He was the light of my life – always smiling and gentle; happy when I answered his Torah questions correctly and forgiving when I did not.

Aside from his Torah scholarship, Grandfather was known in Chicago for his generosity and piety. He never locked his door. Any itinerant Jew, especially the poor and the traveling fundraisers, knew he had a place in the Rubinstein home.

Grandfather was the rabbi of Bnei Reuven Synagogue, then located on Kedvale Avenue in Chicago's West Side Lawndale neighborhood and only loosely affiliated with the Lubavitch movement. Though my grandfather was not a Hasid, he had a relationship with Rabbi Yosef Yitzchak Schneerson, the sixth Rebbe of Lubavitch.

During the Second World War, when my Aunt Judith contracted with a painter to paint his house before Pesach, my grandfather paid him but wouldn't let him do the job. He told my aunt, "While Jews are being killed in Europe, I will not allow myself the pleasure of having my house repainted."

Grandfather had a wonderful sense of humor. An inveterate cigar and pipe-smoker, he once gave a student of his five cents to "please go buy a cigar" for him. The student wanted to honor his teacher, so he bought a twenty-five-cent cigar. After one puff, my grandfather immediately noticed the better quality of the cigar. With a characteristic twinkle in his eye, he called over the student and said: "Here's a dime. Please buy two more of these cigars for me." Decades later, this story was still part of the yeshiva's folklore.

The yeshiva catalogue listed my grandfather as a "senior professor of Talmud." The head of the Jewish studies program at that time was the famed Dr. Meyer Waxman, a great Judaic scholar and author of many books on Jewish literature, history, and other subjects. When shown the catalogue, my grandfather looked at his title and remarked wryly: "If I'm already a senior professor, then what greater title can be given to Dr. Waxman?"

In his later years, Grandfather suffered from cataracts in both his eyes, but he continued to teach Talmud daily, practically from memory. He finally had an operation. (In those days, it was major surgery, requiring weeks of hospitalization.) I remember riding home from the hospital with him. How excitedly he read every street sign and billboard! He marveled at how eyesight was a gift of God. And so it is.

My grandfather also possessed a very melodic voice and served as the cantor every year for the Yom Kippur *Neilah* service. I inherited no such musical talent, as you will discover later in this book.

When Grandfather passed away in October 1944, an enormous crowd of mourners, many of them non-Jews, accompanied him to his final resting place in Chicago's Waldheim Cemetery. My mother and aunts discovered that he owned a life insurance policy worth $10,000, a very princely sum in those days. I remember their discussing how this money would ensure a college education for my cousins and me. They soon discovered, however, that he had assigned the entire policy to the Vaad ha-Hatzala – an organization dedicated to saving as many Jews as possible from the Holocaust.

No one was surprised. It seemed perfectly fitting for him. I remember when he once came home and announced to my mother and aunt, "I left this morning to go to *shul* without taking any money with me. On the way home just now, a stranger approached me and gave me five dollars. Then he disappeared. I was bewildered by the incident.

Two blocks later, a poor man approached me and begged for money to buy food. I gave him the five dollars. I then knew why Heaven had sent me the five dollars."

I am so grateful to have had my grandfather in my life. He has remained my inspiration, role model, and hero. In difficult moments, faced with major problems in my professional and personal life, I have always asked myself: "What would my grandfather have said or done?" And then I've known what to do.

Naturally, my parents were the greatest influence of my youth. Every day, after coming home from public school at 3:15 pm, I would study Torah with my father. By age nine, I was already somewhat proficient in Talmud and even in its commentaries. If I grossly misbehaved at home, my punishment was that he would not teach me that day. It was a fearsome penalty, for I loved studying with him from his old copy of the Talmud, printed on green and blue paper. (Unable to afford the classic Vilna Talmud, he was content with this inexpensive edition.) Those tinted pages remain before my eyes every time I open any volume of the Talmud, even now in my old age.

I briefly attended the Moses Montefiore Talmud Torah, an afterschool program that included relatively high-level study of Mishnah and Talmud. But I was unhappy there: The teacher was a fine Jew but a terrible pedagogue, wielding a cane to maintain discipline. My father and I decided to continue our private study sessions instead.

When I was nine, my grandfather enrolled me in the afternoon preparatory division of Beis Medrash L'Torah, where I studied under Rabbi Nachman Barr, Rabbi Mordechai Schultz, and then Rabbi David Silver, who was a profound influence in my life. In later years, I was friendly with generations of Rabbi Silver's descendants and visited him when I moved to Jerusalem, where he then also lived. He was a master teacher and a very kind and generous pedagogue. He protected me – a short, fat kid, something of a nerd, and younger than everyone else in the class – from bullying.

I also attended Victor F. Lawson Public School in Chicago. The student body was 98 percent Jewish, but the faculty was composed mainly of grim, exacting Irish teachers who drilled us mercilessly in the

The original building of Beis Medrash L'Torah/Hebrew Theological College,
built in 1921 in Chicago

three R's. I was an avid reader from my earliest years, and my mother took me to the public library every week. I completed six grades in four years.

We all had to sing Christmas carols in school, but my mother immunized me early on against these influences. Moreover, because my tone-deaf "singing" threw off the other students, I was ordered not to sing. And I complied, thus beginning my lifelong musical silence.

Though the school was almost all Jewish, we Jews endured bullying and verbal abuse from the few non-Jews. They continually shouted at us: "Go back to Palestine!" In my youth, I was a Palestinian.

There were close to a hundred Jewish boys of my approximate age living on my block, but I was the only Sabbath observer. My mother drilled into me the notion that I was special, that my observance was correct, and that everyone else was sadly mistaken. Only three or four boys attended Shabbat services with their fathers, though seven hundred and fifty men prayed in that *shul*. Almost all of them had already "lost" their children and grandchildren to American assimilation.

But we all played together, and every year we went to the Chicago Cubs baseball game on Chol Hamoed Pesach. No matter how nonobservant they may have been, all Jewish children back then ate matzo on Pesach. So at the ball game Wrigley Field sounded like it was being consumed by termites. Even the ball players heard the crunching in the stands.

In 1946, when I finished sixth grade, my parents wanted to transfer me to a new institution created by the Orthodox community: the Chicago Jewish Academy. Certain Orthodox Jews tried to dissuade them. I remember one such telling my mother, "You'll make him a cripple!" She coolly replied, "But he'll be a *Jewish* cripple."

The Academy began as a junior high and eventually encompassed seventh through twelfth grades. The Jewish studies – mainly Talmud, but also Tanach and Hebrew – were taught in the morning, with secular studies from 1:30 till 5 pm. On Fridays, there were no secular studies. No school on Sundays either. The education was superb, and classes were coed. (A number of girls who grew up to be well-known Hasidic *rebbitzens* and other noted women were my classmates. But this is my biography, not theirs, so I won't reveal their names.)

By the time I reached eighth grade, I was attending yeshiva in the morning and the Academy only in the afternoon. My yeshiva teacher was Rabbi Herzl Kaplan, a product of the Slabodka Yeshiva, a great scholar, and a Renaissance man who knew everything about everything. He taught not only Talmud, but also Tanach, and I completed the books of Jeremiah and Ezekiel under him. The system in the yeshiva was that one stayed with the same teacher for at least two years; that way, we benefited from each teacher in a cumulative fashion.

I loved all my yeshiva teachers, and I always felt they loved me as well. But the Talmud teaches us that it takes forty years to truly appreciate a teacher, and so it is. Looking back, I realize their enormous worth and influence.

On *Parshat Shmini* 5707/1947 I became a *bar mitzvah*. Since my father was the rabbi of a large synagogue, it was a major community event. As mentioned, I couldn't carry a tune even in a paper bag. Nevertheless, Rabbi Silver's father was an outstanding Torah reader (as was his son), and he taught me to read the *Haftorah* from the synagogue's *navi* parchment scroll. My chanting was terrible, but I read all the words perfectly. My *dvar Torah*, which I delivered in Yiddish before a packed congregation, was written for me by Rabbi Kaplan, and it covered a complicated subject in Baba Metzia. I understood what I was saying, and I felt that my *dvar Torah* compensated for my monotonic rendition of the *Haftorah*. A gala Shabbat meal was catered for my *bar mitzvah* in the yeshiva building across the street from my father's *shul*, and there I delivered a speech in English to mark the occasion.

At thirteen, I was confident and had acquired a bit of a reputation as a public speaker. I had spoken publicly a number of times previously, once before a crowd of thousands who came to hear Cantor Pierre Pinchik conduct *Selichot* services in a very large Chicago synagogue. From then on, I was always somewhat excited about speaking publicly, but never fearful. This skill has stood me in good stead throughout my rabbinic career.

Because I was already in high school when my Bar Mitzvah occurred, it effectively ended my childhood. I felt solemnly prepared to embark on my adolescence and a serious career as a yeshiva student.

Chapter 2

My Yeshiva Years

"Life is like chewing gum – a little flavor,
and the rest is chew, chew, chew."

W hen I entered high school, I attended yeshiva from morning until afternoon, then went with my classmates to the Chicago Jewish Academy for secular studies. My *rebbeim* drummed into us that if we weren't earnest about our secular studies, the afternoon hours spent at the Academy would truly be *bitul Torah* – a willful waste of time that otherwise could have been devoted to Torah studies. So I studied Latin for two years, and all the other subjects required by the high school curriculum. The Academy's secular studies department was, as mentioned, excellent, with outstanding teachers and a very serious learning atmosphere.

The administrative head of the yeshiva, its president, was Rabbi Oscar Z. Fasman, who had previously served as a rabbi in Tulsa, Oklahoma, and Ottawa, Canada. He had been a student of my grandfather, Rabbi Rubinstein, in the same yeshiva he now headed. He presided over a change of faculty occasioned by the deaths or retirement to Israel of a number of the older *roshei yeshiva*. Among those who taught in the yeshiva were Rabbi Yisrael Mendel Kaplan (brother of my teacher Rabbi Herzl Kaplan) and Rabbi Mordechai Rogow. Both of these great men had spent the war years escaping from Lithuania and later resided in the Jewish enclave in Kobe, Japan, and then in Shanghai, China. Rabbi

Mordechai Wernick, from the Mir Yeshiva and Shanghai, was the *mashgiach ruchani* (spiritual adviser) and "enforcer" of rules (a most thankless job in an American yeshiva at the time). The very young Rabbi Chaim Kreiswirth was appointed the main *rosh yeshiva* when Rabbi Chaim Korb moved to Israel. Rabbi Kreiswirth was recommended for this post by none other than the chief rabbi of Palestine, Rabbi Isaac Halevi Herzog.

R. Mendel Kaplan

Toward the end of ninth grade, I was placed in Reb Mendel Kaplan's class. Reb Mendel was a disciple of both Rabbi Yerucham Levovitz, the famed *mashgiach* of the Mir Yeshiva, and Rabbi Elchanan Wasserman, *rosh yeshiva* of Baranovitch. I remember the first day he began to teach us. I loved him at first sight, captivated by his blue eyes and reddish beard, great sense of humor, masterful pedagogic techniques, and warm personality. He loved all human beings. Full of understanding, broad-minded and tolerant, he crushed all our childish prejudices against others. He understood the psyche of his young American students, and opened a window to the rich Jewish life of Eastern Europe without denigrating us or our American mores.

Best of all were Reb Mendel's digressions in the midst of teaching Talmud. They touched on all aspects of life and helped shape me as a Jew and a person. Once you studied with Reb Mendel, your outlook on life deepened; your understanding of Jewish values and Torah observance expanded exponentially.

His love and respect for his brother, Rabbi Herzl Kaplan, was palpable and helped teach me an important lesson about family loyalty and harmony. If you asked Reb Mendel a particularly difficult question on the Talmudic text, he would refer you to his brother.

On the frosty Friday nights of the winter, he conducted a class on the weekly *parshah*. Attendance was voluntary, but he purposely limited the roster of who had the right to attend. This tactic naturally made it the most sought-after class in the yeshiva. He would begin at 10 pm and lock the door at 10:01. The room was always filled, and many times the class didn't end until 1 am. It was (as my father always said of Rabbi Kook's Shabbat discourses) "a taste of the World to Come," replete with the warmth and holiness of Shabbat that flooded the crowded room with spirit. My mother was not always so happy about my coming home late at night, but my father rejoiced at my spiritual growth under Reb Mendel's tutelage. I had now become not only my father's son, but his learning partner as well, so to speak, sharing with him Reb Mendel's wisdom.

Reb Mendel's aphorisms have remained with me. I can still hear him say, "*Frum iz a galach* (Only a monk is pious!)" or "Life is like chewing gum – a little flavor, and the rest is chew, chew, chew." He taught me how to really read a newspaper, spotting its unintended lessons in life. And he was a shrewd judge of character, yet never overly cynical or depressing. He seemed to have the right answer for all situations, and his advice was unerringly cogent.

I viewed Reb Mendel as a holy Jew with downright supernatural powers. I always marveled at his ability to leaf through books at random on his desk without missing a beat in teaching Talmud. One such book, an Israeli Jewish history text, accepted as fact that there were two Isaiahs (a favorite gambit of Bible critics and *maskilim*). It not only recorded this "fact" but actually featured a portrait – an artist's rendition of a wild-eyed, bearded, bareheaded Jew of ancient visage – of this "second" Isaiah. So while teaching us a complicated subject in Talmud, Reb Mendel happened to be flipping through this book. He spied the picture of the "second Isaiah," and we all held our breath. Without interrupting his explanation of the Talmud, he calmly flung the volume across our sizable classroom. We watched transfixed as the book shot directly into the wastebasket at the far end of the room. I never again had any doubts about the unity of the book of Isaiah. Reb Mendel had convinced me.

Reb Mendel paid special attention to me. At least, that was how I felt. I now realize that everyone in his class felt that way. I spent two and a half years in his class and never lost contact with him for the rest of his life.

Chicago's Jewish youth groups were connected to Hapoel Hamizrachi, the largest and most active Orthodox organization in the city. I attended the Shabbat afternoon groups for several years, but when I was fourteen, Reb Mendel gently weaned me away from them. I began spending my Shabbat afternoons in the yeshiva and at home studying with my father.

I spent two summers at Camp Moshava, located in Rolling Prairie, Indiana. I didn't really enjoy camping; the lack of privacy made me uncomfortable. So when Reb Mendel recommended summer school instead, and learning with older students in the yeshiva, I happily took him up on it.

Yet the Hapoel Hamizrachi experience provided me with friends and an opportunity to socialize in a religious atmosphere, which helped ameliorate my inherent shyness. (I'm told that social reticence is part of the "only child" syndrome.) It also implanted knowledge and love of the Land of Israel. It nurtured within me a yearning for *aliyah*, which would come to fruition fifty years later.

Letters from my Israeli relatives and Hapoel Hamizrachi sensitized me to the turbulent historical drama unfolding in the newborn State of Israel. All the struggles were real and heartrending, yet despite everything the Jews were returning to their homeland!

I'll never forget the speech delivered by the great Rav of Ponivezh, Rabbi Yosef Shlomo Kahaneman, in the Chicago yeshiva in 1946 or '47. He stated that a number of Jews in Palestine were determined to drive the British out of the country, and had now been imprisoned. And he said with great conviction (and, I thought, prophecy) that these few Jews would undoubtedly succeed. Then he added: "If I had a cadre of Jews who were equally determined to build a Torah state in the Land of Israel, such a Torah state would undoubtedly arise." I have remembered his words all my life. That cadre of idealists has not yet fully arrived – though the State of Israel is decidedly more Torah-oriented today than ever.

I spent eleventh and twelfth grades in the class of Rabbi Rogow, a true *tzaddik*. He was modest, courteous, soft-spoken, and gentle, and his entire being was dedicated to Torah study and teaching. Before fleeing to Shanghai, he had served as a rabbi in the Lithuanian town of Sinaii, known for its meritorious rabbinic figures. He and my father were good friends, and I often eavesdropped on their reminiscences of Lithuania and was amazed by their knowledge of works of Torah that I had never heard of, let alone studied.

Rabbi Rogow taught one class in the morning and one in the evening, and for a while I attended both. Since all the yeshiva *rebbeim* taught in Yiddish, eventually I became proficient in that language, so much so that I felt it was constructed purely for expressing the nuances of Talmud study. Rabbi Rogow taught in the classical Lithuanian analytical style, interspersing the insights of centuries of commentators. We nevertheless completed at least fifty folios of Talmud every year. He urged us to compose short essays in Hebrew on the Talmudic topics of the week. There was a bulletin board outside the main study hall, and there he posted the best essay of the week for the entire yeshiva – faculty and students – to see and study. A number of my essays were posted, beginning my lifelong interest in writing words of Torah.

Every Friday morning, Rabbi Rogow would deliver a *pilpul shiur* – a long, detailed analysis of a subject we had studied (and supposedly mastered) that week. He would also offer a ten-minute homiletical insight into the *parshah* of the week. Ah, he was a master at that. I gained a great deal from him: how to see Midrash and use its insights for sermons and discussions. On Shabbat afternoons, a number of us would walk over to his apartment and study with him. His wife, a niece of the great Rabbi Baruch Ber Leibowitz and an outstanding personality in her own right, would stuff us with her cookies. The warmth and radiance of Shabbat and Torah in that home permeated all our beings, and I believe it helped shape many of us into rabbis, teachers, and Jewish leaders the world over.

I've always felt especially blessed that I had such marvelous Torah teachers. I was the youngest in the yeshiva and many other students were already past high school. Nevertheless, I had good friends and great social interactions with everyone.

After high school, I was awarded a full scholarship to Roosevelt College, based on my entrance exam and high school record. Since I was in the yeshiva all day until 5:30 pm, I attended only night school and summer sessions. Roosevelt College was a very liberal, left-wing institution, and a number of my teachers were avowed Communists and atheists who looked askance at yeshiva students. I had many a sharp debate with some of these professors on matters of religion and differing value systems. To their credit, they never punished me for my "reactionary views" when it came to grading me at the end of the semester. I was pretty much an A student in college, but no subject captivated me. I majored in education by default, but my heart and mind were really in my Torah studies. Though my day was long – starting yeshiva at 7 am, and returning home from college at 10:30 pm to begin my homework – I was quite happy.

Rabbi Kreiswirth, the *rosh yeshiva*, fostered my commitment to Torah study. In his early thirties, handsome – with a small, French-style, trimmed beard – and dressed in bright, modern suits and colorful ties, he was charismatic and dynamic. He was also a Talmudic genius, possessed of a photographic memory, who inspired devotion and emulation among his students. He was a world-class orator as well, and from listening to him I gained many insights into the art of public speaking and the use of Talmudic anecdotes in lectures and sermons.

Rabbi Kreiswirth became my mentor, trusted adviser, and role model. He played a constant, significant role in my life until his death. In my opinion, his interpersonal skills and innate abilities influenced his students more than his Talmudic lectures, in which his soaring genius – expressed in a Polish Yiddish dialect – was often over our heads. A powerful personality, he shaped the lives and ideals of his students. He demanded that we help rebuild the Jewish world – especially the Torah world – after the terrible events of World War II.

Rabbi Kreiswirth introduced us to towering Torah personalities passing through Chicago. Somehow he corralled them all to come speak to us on Friday mornings. Thus, I met and heard Rabbis Eliyahu Kitov (Monktofsky), Binyamin Mintz (of Poalei Agudat Yisrael), Meir Karelitz (secretary to the Chofetz Chaim), and Yaakov Kamenetsky (Rabbi Kreiswirth's wife's uncle and *rosh yeshiva* of Mesivta Torah Vodaath in Brooklyn), among a host of other fascinating people. Rabbi Kreiswirth knew everyone there was to know in the Torah world. And we, his students, benefited from his superb networking.

At age nineteen, finishing my second year in college, I was accepted into the *semichah* program in the yeshiva. Not everyone was. According to an anecdote that made the rounds in the yeshiva for decades, a young man was refused, and his mother personally appealed the decision to the dean of the yeshiva. She maintained that her son was the most pious student in the yeshiva. How could he be excluded from the program? The dean told her: "Madam, for piety one merits the World to Come, but not *semichah!*"

The program required two years of intensive study of *Shulchan Aruch* – mainly *Yoreh Deah* (laws of *kashrut*, family purity, and mourning) and *Orach Chaim* (laws of prayer, Shabbat, holidays, daily ritual, and synagogue practice) – plus some homiletics, speech training and practical rabbinics, philosophy, and history. The main teacher was Rabbi David Kaganoff, an outstanding Talmudic scholar from the Slabodka Yeshiva in Lithuania, and a pulpit rabbi on the northwest side of Chicago. He was a demanding teacher, yet very kind and caring.

Rabbi Kaganoff was very kind to me. When I was about to become engaged, I had no money to buy an engagement ring. My jeweler neighbor assured me that I could get a suitable ring for $300. Rabbi Kaganoff came to the rescue. He invited me to speak to his congregation over the High Holidays of 5715/1954. My pay would be exactly $300. Naturally, I accepted the offer. In addition to the fee, I wanted the experience of addressing a sizable congregation on the High Holidays. It was perfect. The gracious hospitality of Rabbi Kaganoff and his wife over the holidays was a memorable bonus.

During my yeshiva years, I spent many a lunch hour in the yeshiva library. The library was a magnificent room and had a librarian on duty, Mrs. Leah Mishkin, who was the daughter of Rabbi Nissan Yablonsky, the first *rosh yeshiva*. It was there I began reading books on Jewish history, in English and Hebrew, and Mrs. Mishkin always found interesting journals and articles on Judaic studies for me. I did not realize what an effect those hours in the yeshiva library would have upon me in later life.

The younger students in the yeshiva were close to my age, and I made every effort to maintain contact with them, though the *semichah* students were somewhat cut off from the rest. Many of my friends from those years later became luminaries in the Jewish world. The list reads like a *Who's Who* of Jewish leadership: Rabbi Nosson Zvi Finkel, head of the famed Mir Yeshiva of Jerusalem; Dr. Avigdor (Victor) Bonchek, noted therapist and expert on Rashi's Bible commentary; Dr. Aron Twerski, a dean at Hofstra Law School in New York; Dr. Twerski's twin brother, Rabbi Michel Twerski, a Hasidic *rebbe* in Milwaukee and an outstanding force in the *kiruv* movement in America; Rabbi Dr. Abraham

(Shiya) Twerski, the famed author, lecturer, psychiatrist, and addiction expert; Rabbi Reuven Aberman, dean of students at Rabbi Isaac Elchanan Theological Seminary (part of Yeshiva University in New York) and later a prominent educator in Israel; Rabbi Shlomo Merzel, head of the Horev education network in Jerusalem; Rabbi Milton Polin, well-known pulpit rabbi and president of the Rabbinical Council of America; Rabbi Yehuda Copperman, founder and longtime head of the Michlala women's college in Jerusalem; Rabbi Aryeh Rottman, founder and head of Yeshiva Mercaz HaTorah in Jerusalem; Rabbi David Kalefski, *rosh yeshiva* of Ner Israel Rabbinical College in Baltimore; Rabbis Gershon and Mordechai Swimmer, both renowned Torah educators in Israel; Rabbi David Lehrfield of Miami, one of the world's foremost experts in *gittin*; Rabbi David Fox, a *rosh kollel* and educator in Israel; and Rabbi Moshe Litoff, a rabbi in Chicago and later dean of students at Bar-Ilan University in Israel.

As you can see, the yeshiva in Chicago possessed an extraordinarily outstanding, individualistic, and varied student body. Through these students, the yeshiva contributed greatly to the rebirth of Orthodoxy and Torah study throughout the Jewish world. I have always felt most fortunate to have been in the right place – Beis Medrash L'Torah in Chicago, at the right time – 1944 to 1955.

Surrounded by the intellectual ferment of my fellow students and outstanding *rebbeim*, I studied *Yoreh Deah* very thoroughly and passed the difficult oral, closed-book exams. In 1955, at age twenty-one, I received my *semichah*, becoming the seventh consecutive generation in my family to be ordained. However, the official ceremony didn't take place until 1959, when there was a significant number of *musmachim* (recently ordained rabbis) to present to the Jewish public in Chicago.

By '59, the yeshiva had relocated to Skokie, a northern suburb of Chicago. Though the move was necessary, it had a somewhat negative effect. Rabbi Mendel Kaplan left to teach in Philadelphia, Rabbi Kreiswirth became the rabbi of Antwerp, and Rabbi Wernick also left the yeshiva.

By the time Rabbi Rogow passed away, the golden age of the Chicago yeshiva was over. The yeshiva never replicated the faculty, student body, and spirit it possessed in the late 1940s and early 1950s.

The yeshiva 1954 ordination class and faculty. Front row, right to left: Rabbis Herzl Kaplan, Chaim Kreiswirth, David Kaganoff, Oscar Z. Fasman, Chaim D. Regensberg, Mordechai Rogow, and Joseph Babad

A great change occurred in the geography and demography of Chicago Jewry at that same time. The Lawndale neighborhood, where a huge proportion of Chicago's Jews lived, changed slowly but inexorably into an Afro-American area. Violent crime and petty theft became commonplace there, and the Jews fled the neighborhood that had been home to them for over forty years. This transformation coincided with the meteoric rise of the Conservative movement in American Jewry. Many of Lawndale's Orthodox synagogues moved to new neighborhoods, happily morphing into Conservative institutions. A number of transplanted congregations dubbed themselves "traditional," abandoning separate seating for men and women but maintaining Orthodox prayer rituals. Orthodox rabbis served as their spiritual leaders.

The number of truly Orthodox synagogues in Chicago shrank dramatically, and my father's merged with a much smaller congregation in the East Rogers Park neighborhood. Several non-*mechitzah* synagogues had asked him to become their rabbi, but he refused. He told me: "I saw Rabbi Shimon Shkop with my own eyes! These younger rabbis never saw him, so they can somehow rationalize serving in such synagogues."

"I don't see much of a future for the Orthodox rabbinate in America," my father told me. "I don't want you to be a rabbi in a traditional or Conservative synagogue, and I have no money or business to leave you. You'll have to make your own way. We have a Ratzki-born distant relative, Hyman Abrams, who is a successful lawyer here in Chicago. He has promised me that if you finish law school and pass the Illinois bar exam, he will give you a job in his firm. I want you to go to law school and take up his offer."

I gulped, and thought about it long and hard. In the end, as usual, I followed my father's advice.

I applied to the University of Chicago Law School, a very prestigious place indeed. Not only was I accepted, I was awarded a full scholarship. But the rub was that I would no longer be able to attend the yeshiva, since there were no night classes at the law school. So I applied to the DePaul University College of Law and was accepted. DePaul had a full night school schedule, which would allow me to remain in the yeshiva until 5:30 pm. The difference between the University of Chicago and DePaul was explained to me by the dean of the latter: "The University of Chicago accepts only seventy-five students into its first-year law school class, but expects all seventy-five to complete the program and pass the bar. DePaul accepts three hundred students into its first-year law school class, but expects only seventy-five to complete their studies and pass the bar." The DePaul night school classes were taught by excellent professors – some became federal judges – and the students were serious, older, and committed. However, true to the dean's prediction, most of my classmates dropped out.

DePaul is a Roman Catholic institution, and its atmosphere and faculty provided a stark contrast with the liberal, progressive, and relaxed atmosphere at Roosevelt College. Paradoxically, I felt much more at home in the Catholic school than in the atheistic/agnostic, hedonistic liberal arts college.

Yet DePaul exposed me to the real world, to non-Jews who disliked me simply because I was Jewish. Roosevelt College had many Jewish students, so to a certain extent I never felt strange there. At DePaul, the overwhelming majority of law students were Roman Catholic and somewhat bigoted. There were only two black students and one woman in our very large class, and they were pretty much as isolated as I was.

Nevertheless, law school was, all in all, a positive experience for me. I did fairly well there, even winning a prize for the best freshman grades. And I'm grateful for my law education. It helped train me in analysis and research, and greatly improved my writing. Because of my double schedule with the yeshiva, I learned to multitask before the word was invented.

When it came to graduation, the two other Orthodox Jews and I faced a dilemma. The school was celebrating a special anniversary that year, so the graduation would be held in the largest Roman Catholic cathedral in Chicago, with the cardinal of Chicago himself handing out the diplomas. Courtesy and tradition dictated that each recipient kiss the cardinal's ring, or perform some other act of servitude. And in order to sit for the Illinois bar exam and gain a license to practice law, one had to bring a document from law school stating that he had attended his graduation ceremony, or been lawfully excused from attending.

We discussed how to resolve the dilemma. One of my colleagues suggested that we each obtain doctor's notes stating that we were ill on graduation day. I rejected the idea as untruthful and impractical. I recommended that we go to the dean of the law school and simply tell him the truth. When we did finally go, he was most understanding and issued us the necessary documents to sit for the bar exam. He explained that barely a month earlier his predecessor, a nephew and namesake of president and former chief justice William Howard Taft, had died. Dean Taft had built the law school and nurtured it for decades, and he was its original claim to fame. Yet he was not a Roman Catholic, so his funeral did not conform to Catholic rituals and sensitivity. Therefore, none of the Catholic professors at the law school attended. So the current dean understood our position and was most accommodating.

And I learned an important, lifelong lesson: The most successful lie is always the truth.

Chapter 3

An Ideal Marriage

"We knew the Lord had granted us a gift."

I was always the youngest in my class, and since all my friends were three to four years older, many were already looking to get married. Though only eighteen, I followed their lead, assessing the girls I knew in terms of marriage. There were some wonderful girls in our high school, but none of them considered me marriage material. The Lord apparently thought otherwise and had plans for me.

When I was barely approaching my nineteenth birthday, Rabbi Kreiswirth asked me to travel to Detroit to meet a dude ranch owner from Arizona and propose that he sponsor a *kollel* to be located at his ranch. The scheme seemed preposterous, but I dutifully agreed. I took a Greyhound bus to Detroit and met with the rancher, who immediately dismissed the idea. It was Friday, and too late for me to return to Chicago for Shabbat. I had cousins in Detroit, Bertha Merzon and her husband, Manuel, so I invited myself to their home for Shabbat. Friday night, after the meal, I sat down to study Talmud. Everyone, even my relatives, thought I was older, since I was already a sophomore. "All the religious young people are meeting socially tonight at a home near here," my cousin informed me. "Why don't you go too?" I told her I'd feel strange not knowing anyone there; I would rather stay home and study.

But Bertha was a persistent lady – all the women in my family were and are strong personalities – and literally dragged me to the get-together.

At that time, there was a prominent Orthodox leader in the Detroit community: Lithuanian-born Rabbi Leizer Levin. His daughter, Jackie, was his youngest child, a student at Wayne State University in Detroit. She had come to the Friday evening gathering, and we were introduced. For me, it was love at first sight. It seemed strange that Rabbi Levin's daughter should be called Jackie, but that only fueled my interest in her. We had a wonderful conversation, sharing the consequences of being victims of strange first names. Her name was Yocheved, which a well-meaning neighbor (an experienced immigration officer) had authoritatively translated into English as Jackabed. So she always called herself Jackie, to avoid embarrassment.

Little did I know that a girlfriend of Jackie's was a neighbor of mine in Chicago who had told her we would be a perfect match. So Jackie had already heard about me and expressed interest in meeting me. Looking back, I guess you could say I was set up. Was that why Bertha was so insistent about my going to this event?

Right to left: R. Leizer Levin, Jackie, and
R. Levin's second wife Chana

Simchat Torah. In his great faith and self-control, my father-in-law
through Shmini Atzeret and Simchat Torah without displaying any
. The day of the funeral was very emotional for all of us as well as
he Detroit Jewish community, as everyone admired and loved her.
brother-in-law, Rabbi Avraham Chaim Levin, and his wife, Esther,
ved to Detroit from Cleveland and lived with my father-in-law for
next year, until he remarried.

Rabbi Levin's second wife was Chana Heschel, a descendant of
asidic masters and also a very aristocratic woman. Chana had been mar-
ed but had no children. Possessed of great intellect and broad Jewish
nd worldly knowledge, she had served as a librarian in a Jewish library
n Kiev during Stalin's rule in the 1920s. She escaped to the Land of Israel
nd later to America. Chana and my father-in-law lived together for over
twenty-eight years in harmony and mutual respect. She certainly added
years to his life through her care and loyalty, and she was an omnipresent force in our family. She predeceased Rabbi Levin by a number of
years, and is buried with her family in Petach Tikva.

After Chana's death, our nephew, Rabbi Shmuel Yehuda Levin,
his wife, and their young children moved in with my father-in-law. Their
care enabled him to be an active and important member of the Detroit
Jewish community until the last weeks of his long life. He must have been
at least ninety-six when he died. Rabbi Levin is buried in the Ponivezh
cemetery in Bnei Brak, near the graves of Rav Eliezer Menachem Shach
and Rav Yechezkel Levenstein. My mother-in-law was reinterred on Har
Hazeitim in Jerusalem (as was my mother, in our family plot there).

Rabbi Yisrael Meir Levin, another nephew, then moved to
Detroit, taking up residence with his family in his grandfather's house.
He also became the rabbi in his grandfather's synagogue – so the Detroit
Jewish community has had a Rabbi Levin in a leadership role for almost
seventy-five years.

Rabbi Leizer Levin belonged to the world of the great men
of *Mussar* (Jewish ethics) – inwardly pious, gracious, kind, sensitive
scholars who spent their lives purifying and refining their character and
behavior. Being a member of the Levin household was one of the major
blessings in my life.

In any case, we agreed to go to a concert downtown on Saturday
night. I borrowed a car from my cousin (she was already planning the
wedding!) and picked up Jackie at her home. I met Rabbi Levin and
his wife (Sarah Menucha née Hoffenberg), and we had a very pleasant,
relaxed conversation. Rabbi Levin remembered my grandfather, Rabbi
Rubinstein, who had visited Detroit often. And Manuel Merzon, a lawyer and a truly holy person, was quite close to Rabbi Levin.

When we got into the car to drive downtown, I innocently asked
Jackie for directions. Jackie had no sense of direction. She replied: "Just
get behind the Dexter bus and follow it. It will get us downtown." I was
fascinated by her. She thought I was five years older than I actually was,
and would never have gone out with me had she known the truth. By
the time I admitted my age to her a year later, we were in love; age no
longer mattered.

During our two-year courtship, Jackie came to Chicago a number of times, and I went to Detroit on several occasions. I don't think
we saw each other more than fifteen times during the entire period. A
long-distance call was an event in those days, so we phoned only several
times a year. But we corresponded twice a week, and that's how we got
to know each other.

When I visited Detroit in November 1954, Rabbi Levin saw we
were happy and discouraged a longer courtship. Jackie hesitated because
she had an older sister, Itta Bracha, who was not yet married. But Rabbi
Levin gently prevailed upon her, and we had a formal *tena'im* (engagement) dinner at the now defunct Hamilton Hotel in Chicago that January. I gave her an engagement ring (which I'd bought through the good
offices of Rabbi Kaganoff, as mentioned earlier). Rabbi Rogow was the
main speaker at the dinner, and all my teachers and friends at the yeshiva,
my father's congregants, and our relatives attended.

We agreed to be married in June. By then, Jackie would finish
college and I would receive my *semichah* and complete my second year
of law school. During our wedding feast, in Detroit, I delivered a thirty-
minute Talmudic *dvar Torah*, as was customary in those distant days.

We moved into a three-room apartment in Chicago that was
quite cozy, reasonable in rent, and far enough from my parents to make
it comfortable for all concerned, though we spent most Shabbatot with

them. Jackie taught at the local day school, and my parents helped us out until I finished law school and began working. I graduated in January 1956 and sat for the bar exam a few months later. I passed it rather easily.

Quite honestly, when we first married Jackie barely knew how to boil water. But she became a gourmet cook and baker, and was a fastidious housekeeper. Our home was always clean, neat, and filled with warmth, laughter, and love. Our first child, Miriam, was born in May 1956, while I was studying for the bar. It was then that we faced the first of a series of major challenges in our first decade of married life.

When we married, we had not known that we had a blood incompatibility, which threatened the very life of our baby. She required an immediate blood transfusion (something unheard of in my generation), and it was touch and go for a day or two. Jackie had her father's sense of calm and faith, while I was shaken and distraught. Faith is a wonderful thing that rabbis talk about, but it is a revelation to actually see it in action in difficult times and circumstances. Jackie had faith enough for both of us. Her calm steadfastness was the backbone of our family life, seeing us through the raising of our children and the vagaries of career.

A year after Miriam was born, Jackie suffered a miscarriage. Our son, Chaim Zvi (named after my beloved grandfather), was born a year later, and also had to stay in the hospital for ten days after his birth, because of a reparable surface abnormality. His circumcision took place in the hospital, with the *mohel* closely observed by the resident urologists. A year later, our daughter Dena was born. She, too, needed the blood transfusion/replacement procedure to which we had become accustomed. When we brought her home, Miriam commented, "I don't know why we needed another baby. We haven't used up the one we already have."

My mother-in-law was a beautiful and aristocratic woman. I never heard a cross word from her. Fifteen years before our marriage, she had suffered from breast cancer. Though it had been in remission for so many years, it returned after our marriage, until it was uncontrollable. She passed away on Hoshana Rabbah 5720/1959. The funeral was in Detroit on the day

My daughter Miriam and her family, the Gettingers (2012)

Right to left: My son R. Chaim Zvi, my grandson Yechiel, me, and Mira

Jackie had a routine x-ray when she was expecting our fourth child. (Believe it or not, they still x-rayed pregnant women in those days.) To our utter shock, the x-ray revealed a lymphatic disease – Hodgkin's. At that time, the cure rate was about 5 percent.

The doctors wanted to abort the pregnancy and begin treating the disease. My wife and I discussed the matter and agreed that we wanted the baby, hoping for God's grace. Our daughter Sara (Sori) was born at the beginning of July 1960. We discovered a doctor by the name of Joppa who was experimenting with intensive radiation treatment for Hodgkin's patients. He was very encouraging when we met with him, and we decided to pursue his treatment. He warned us that the x-rays would scar the lungs, but he felt it was worth the risk. Jackie underwent these treatments for ten months. The side effects were completely disabling, so my mother helped care for the baby and the other small children. But by the grace of God, the treatments worked, and my wife made medical history and remained completely cured. Jackie indeed suffered from scarred lungs for the rest of her life. But she had a "rest of her life" because of those treatments!

Me, my daughters Dena and Sori, and grandchildren

Thirty-five years later, she was interviewed at Sloan-Kettering Medical Center in New York and was told that she was the longest-surviving recipient of such treatments. But for the rest of our married life, that disease was the elephant in the room. We never spoke about it; we just lived a loving, special married life. But we knew the Lord had granted us a gift. This realization shaped many of our decisions and attitudes. We had a marvelous, passionate marriage for fifty-one years, with very few bumps along the way. Jackie was God's greatest gift to me.

Chapter 4

Taking My Place in the Community

"Even my years in university and law school did not
adequately prepare me for the real world."

I passed the Illinois bar exam and was admitted to practice in November 1956. My father had arranged employment for me with the Abrams and Lynn law firm. The firm had offices on LaSalle Street in downtown Chicago and in a Polish neighborhood in South Chicago. I worked mainly at the downtown office. I learned my craft quickly and appeared regularly in the municipal and federal courts downtown. I also saw the seamier side of the practice – witnessing gifts being lavished upon the clerks of certain judges from whom our firm enjoyed scheduling and procedural favors.

My salary was a paltry fifty dollars a week, but together with my wife's income from teaching at the local day school, we somehow managed. Though the firm's partners knew I was an observant Jew, they continually pressed me to be available on Saturday for emergencies. They pointed out that they had represented observant Jews, even rabbis, who had called them on Saturday when monetary matters were involved. I swallowed hard and made it clear that I would never appear at the office on Saturdays, nor would I answer my phone, no matter what the legal "emergency" may be.

Another former yeshiva student, Manuel J. Finkel, was working for a law firm in the same LaSalle Street building where I worked. We represented opposing clients in some matters and were in charge of pro-rations[1] in real-estate closings. But we studied Torah together often and became fast and lifelong friends.

The real world is a shocking place for someone coming out of a dozen years of safe shelter in a yeshiva. Even my years in university and law school did not adequately prepare me for the real world, where Jewish values practically did not exist – even for observant Jews – in everyday dealings with money, power, and ego. Yet I was married and now had a child; I had to put food on the table. So I dug in and practiced law to the best of my ability. I began working very long hours and was worn down physically and mentally. After a few months, I developed mono-nucleosis and was hospitalized for two weeks. Thank God, that was my only hospitalization for the next fifty-five years.

Over time, I acquired clients – initially, observant Jews who knew my family – and I brought their fees into the firm while I handled their legal matters, especially in real estate and probate law. I developed a good reputation, especially in the rather small observant Jewish community in Chicago. I was given almost all the real-estate work in our firm, and I gained a grasp of real-estate investment, mortgages, leveraging, trusts, and syndication.[2]

I began to consider setting up my own law practice. My friend Manuel Finkel was considering the same. Encouraging each other, we agreed to strike out on our own. We opened an office together, but each of us had his own practice. We rented a nice suite at One North LaSalle Street and took the plunge. Manny Finkel was a much better lawyer

---

1. Taxes, rent, and other collected monies are prorated – distributed – between the buyer and seller of real estate upon the closing of the transaction. These prorations often involve contentious negotiations.
2. Syndication means putting together a group of investors to purchase a certain property, with the syndicator receiving a fee or a piece of the property for his efforts.

than I was, as well as a shrewder judge of people, and I happily played second fiddle.

I met a successful real-estate broker, also a former student at the yeshiva, who began providing me with opportunities to buy properties in Chicago. I started syndicating these properties, and people begged me to invest their money. I also formed a real-estate management company in partnership with a Hebrew school teacher, which began generating steady income. This "partnership" was rather ill-fated, since I did almost all the work, but I let it run its six-year course. I was starting to earn real money. I purchased a townhouse in West Rogers Park, and a few years later I built a home in the Peterson Park neighborhood. People thought I was much richer than I was.

Thanks to this reputation, I became acquainted with many heads of yeshivot in America and Israel who were constantly raising funds for their institutions. I met Rabbi Aaron Kotler in 1953 when I accompanied my father on a visit to Rabbi Kotler's then-very small yeshiva in Lakewood, New Jersey. He told my father that he hoped to eventually have over a hundred students. (Of course, as of this writing, the Lakewood yeshiva's student body numbers in the many thousands.) I was once in my office when my secretary buzzed me, stating that there was a rabbi

Delivering a *shiur* at Lakewood yeshiva's Beth Medrash Govoha 60 years later

calling. Picking up the phone, I heard a voice say in Yiddish, "This is Kotler. Last year you gave me ten dollars. I am old and weaker, and I apologize that I cannot come visit you personally. Please send me the ten dollars this year by mail."

This is a fairly accurate picture of Orthodox Jewish life in the 1950s. It was a desperate time for Jewry in general, but most certainly for the outnumbered and outgunned Orthodox Jewish community.

A number of distinguished rabbis stayed in our home while they raised funds in Chicago. Rabbi Hillel Vitkin of the Novardok yeshiva (now called Yeshivat Beit Hillel) in Bnei Brak stayed with us for over a week. I remember driving him to Midway Airport in Chicago to catch a flight to New York on a Monday morning, and the traffic was horrendous. I told him we would never make the plane; it would be better to return home and catch another flight the next day. He gently demurred, asked me not to worry, and told me to just keep driving. We arrived at the airport twenty minutes after the scheduled departure time, but miraculously the plane was still at the gate. The door of the aircraft was mysteriously jammed and somehow would not close. Once Rabbi Vitkin boarded, the door closed easily and securely.

I was most impressed.

We had the privilege of hosting many other remarkable Jews in Chicago. These experiences strengthened my faith and enhanced my appreciation of great people.

During my years as a lawyer, I was also a "Shabbat Rav." An old congregation from the Lawndale district had relocated to the new Jewish neighborhood, and it had no rabbi. Many young people and couples had joined the synagogue, but it was still controlled by the older members (though many no longer attended). The younger group asked me to serve as part-time rabbi, and the older group agreed. I was only in my early twenties, but I taught numerous classes – especially for teenagers – and was quite satisfied. I drew a very modest salary from the congregation, and I continued to practice law. I was very busy and not home much. In retrospect, I realize how unfair that was to my wife, though she complained little.

After a year, I was firmly entrenched in the congregation, and learned a powerful lesson in *shul* politics. The younger group was composed mainly of my contemporaries and friends. It was clear to me that the synagogue would really take off if they were in charge. They attempted to gain control of the synagogue board, but the older group rallied and defeated them. So the younger group left the *shul*. The older group asked me to stay on, but I decided to serve as the unofficial rabbi of the small *minyan* formed by my friends. I taught classes and spoke on Shabbat. I received no salary, and I was very concerned about supporting my growing family. Yet even then I thought of myself more as a rabbi than as a lawyer.

Jackie and I were very involved in community affairs. There was now a cadre of young people trying to build (or rebuild) a vibrant Orthodox Jewish community in Chicago. Jackie headed a group that promoted family purity among young couples. The group also raised considerable sums to refurbish the *mikvah*, and eventually built a new one in the newer Jewish neighborhood then developing in Chicago. (One of the main activists in building that *mikvah* was Isidore Kaplan, also a Chicago attorney.)

My wife also taught in the Arie Crown Hebrew Day School, and she did an outstanding job. William Rosenblum was the driving force behind the school. Rosenblum owned the largest Hebrew bookstore in Chicago, and I was a regular customer of his. He always found books that he claimed I simply had to have. He aided me greatly in building up my rabbinic library, which peaked at quite a few thousand volumes. He was also a client of mine on minor legal matters.

Rosenblum wanted me to be active in Arie Crown, but I was more interested in the older and less "modern" Bais Yaakov Hebrew Parochial School. The Meisels brothers, refugee Hasidic *rebbes* in Chicago, were clients of mine – one became a very successful nursing home operator – and I helped them strengthen and develop Bais Yaakov. My children attended that school, as did theirs. Some of my daughters' classmates became leading Hasidic *rebbes*. Times and mores were different then.

Every Sunday morning, the head of the transportation company that provided bus service for the school would park at my front door and not leave until he was paid for the previous week. Since the school always lacked funds, and paying the teachers was my first priority, I often paid him out of my own pocket just to get some peace.

I remained active in running Bais Yaakov until my departure from Chicago in 1964. The school still exists, almost fifty years later, though it has been outflanked on the right by a *cheder*-type institution ironically named for one of the Meisels'. Arie Crown also still exists, as does the Chicago Jewish Academy (now the Ida Crown Jewish Academy) and the Hebrew Theological College (better known as the Skokie Yeshiva). Thus, a piece of me remains in Chicago, and I still consider it my *"alter heim"* – the "old country" that helped shape me. The Chicago I knew pretty much no longer exists socially or religiously, but I always feel a tug of emotion when the plane lands at O'Hare Airport. I am flooded by memories of my first thirty years of life spent there.

But enough of this *schmaltz*.

In early 1960, I received a phone call from Rabbi Mordechai Katz, head of Telshe Yeshiva in Cleveland, to please come to Cleveland to discuss an important matter with him. I had no idea what he wanted, but I went anyway. My wife's brother, Rabbi Avraham Chaim Levin, taught in the yeshiva, as did Rabbi Chaim Dov Keller, who was married to Debbie, my wife's oldest sister. I looked forward to a pleasant family visit if nothing else. My two brothers-in-law and I always found each other interesting.

Rabbi Katz wanted to establish a branch of Telshe Yeshiva in Chicago in the fall, and asked for my help. He told me to expect the usual opposition to anything new in an established Jewish community; but he was convinced that Telshe Yeshiva could and would succeed in Chicago. The yeshiva would be headed by my brother-in-law and Rabbi Chaim Shmelczer. The first students would be a group of twelve young men whom he would send from Cleveland. I reluctantly agreed to be the point man for the project, sensing the difficulties that lay ahead. I was only twenty-six, and had grave doubts about whether I was up to the task.

I plunged into the work of opening the yeshiva that September. A committee of lay leaders was formed, some of them clients of mine. Through their efforts, a venue was obtained on the lower floor of the Adas Bnei Israel synagogue. Isidore Kaplan was again instrumental, as was Sam Raitzik, both prominent members of that synagogue. As I had foreseen, however, there was great opposition to a Telshe Yeshiva in Chicago. On the morning of the yeshiva's scheduled opening, that opposition led the synagogue president to padlock the building shut. I went to his house and had breakfast with him, cajoling him into giving me the keys.

The yeshiva began to function. I often prayed there, and every weekday had a very early morning learning session with Rabbi David Oppen, an excellent Torah scholar. I was also privileged to attend a learning group every Shabbat afternoon at the home of Rabbi Chaim Zimmerman, one of the outstanding Talmudic geniuses of the time. Rabbi Zimmerman was then teaching at the Skokie Yeshiva. He was a friend of my parents', and I was allowed to sit among the august group of older scholars who studied with him. I gained a great deal; Rabbi Zimmerman expanded my view, scope, and knowledge of Torah immensely.

I also became a close friend of Rabbi Shmelczer's. Though the Telshe Yeshiva struggled financially during its first years, through his heroic efforts it took root and flourished. In its second year, Rabbi Keller and family moved to Chicago to join Rabbis Levin and Shmelczer in heading the yeshiva. Jackie was delighted to have her brother and sister as neighbors of ours in Chicago. And if my wife was delighted, so was I.

Receiving an award at the first annual banquet of Telshe Yeshiva Chicago from R. Mordechai Katz, *rosh yeshiva* of Telshe Yeshiva Cleveland (right) and R. Aron Eisenberg, chairman of Telshe Yeshiva Chicago (center) (1963)

The Telshe Yeshiva in Chicago has since become an important fixture on the American yeshiva landscape. It was gratifying for me to be the guest speaker at its fiftieth-anniversary banquet in Chicago in December 2010.

My law practice and real-estate ventures prospered. I drove a big Oldsmobile 88, lived in a nice house, and paid my taxes and tuition on time. But I was becoming disenchanted with my profession. A lawyer usually sees people at their worst, and witnessing such behavior really began to wear on me. This was especially true with many of my Orthodox clients, who presented themselves as paragons of probity and piety. It took great effort on my part not to become cynical. In one instance, I represented a great Talmudic scholar determined to purchase a certain nursing home in Chicago. Another Talmudic scholar opposed him, and the dispute turned bitter and prolonged. Both men harassed me day and night. Though my client eventually won, the whole affair left me sick at heart.

Despite my successful law practice, I did not enjoy the confrontations and arguments that are the grist for the legal mill. And my wife's illness weighed heavily upon me. In addition, the real-estate market was entering one of its periodic downturns, and some of my projects – a medical center and an apartment building under construction – ran into financial trouble. Investors long accustomed to 10 percent returns complained bitterly about receiving 4 or 5 percent. It was tempting to create a Ponzi scheme in order to boost returns. I resisted that temptation, thereby saving my life and family.

I saw a newspaper ad for the sale of a small tool, die, and metal stamping business. I investigated and saw that it was really a good opportunity, so I convinced Manny Finkel and Irving Nathan – a successful accountant and friend – to go in with me. I cut back on my law practice and real estate dealings and personally managed the business. I taught myself how to read blueprints for the very small, specialized, and complicated parts that our company manufactured for such large firms as Bell and Howell (cameras), Beltone (hearing aids), and Webcor (tape recorders), and for light aircraft as well. It was a low-volume business but immensely lucrative, with net profits approaching one-third of the gross volume billed. I spent most of my time at the business, and I learned how to deal with purchasing agents, die makers, alcoholic workers, Thanksgiving and Christmas parties, delivery deadlines, and government health and safety inspectors. It really gave me a broad sweep of experience. I learned of the workings of the world in real time with maximum practicality, completing the education that began when I started practicing law.

But my main fulfillment came from my daily Talmud learning and my Shabbat classes and sermons – and above all else, from my family.

Chapter 5

Switching Gears

"He spoke of a coming revolution in American Jewish life;
of a growing and vital Orthodoxy."

Aside from the two very influential speeches I heard from Rabbi Herzog and Rabbi Kahaneman (the Ponivezher Rav), two addresses delivered at banquets in the 1950s impacted my life's ambitions and thoughts.

The first was by Herman Wouk, the Pulitzer Prize-winning author, playwright, and screenwriter. He was an observant Jew who had made good in the outside world – a rarity in his time. Back then, the Jewish world believed that no Orthodox Jew could succeed in American life without sacrificing Torah observance and beliefs. The prevalent assumption was that one had to blend in to the general American lifestyle and mores in order to achieve fame and fortune. Considered an anachronism, Orthodox Jews were encouraged to maintain a low profile and never rock the boat.

(I was a member of the Decalogue Society of Lawyers in Chicago, a group of Chicago Jewish lawyers, and was shocked when the group's annual dinner was blatantly non-kosher. Both Manny Finkel and I protested. When we were curtly told to mind our own business, we publicly resigned. Of course, nothing of apparent value came of our action.)

In such an anti-Orthodox climate, Herman Wouk delivered a

forty-five-minute oratorical gem in defense of Torah study and observance to a mainly non-observant audience. He warned that his listeners would have no Jewish descendants if they themselves did not adopt a more Jewish lifestyle. The audience was stunned, for the Orthodox rabbis of the day dared not be so blunt. For the first time in a long time, I felt that Orthodoxy had a chance to succeed in a big way in America.

I always have been grateful to Wouk for that speech and for his great book *This Is My God*. I found this work very useful in my rabbinic career; I must have given away dozens of copies to Jews who knew nothing of their faith but felt some inner pull to at least find out what they were abandoning.

The second speech, delivered at a banquet for Beis Medrash L'Torah in the early 1950s, was by Rabbi Pinchas M. Teitz of Elizabeth, New Jersey. Most European rabbis used speaking engagements to bemoan the state of American Jewry, especially in comparison to the glory days of Eastern European Jewish life. Not Rabbi Teitz. He spoke of a coming revolution in American Jewish life; of a growing and vital Orthodoxy; of the triumph of the day school and yeshiva movements; and he predicted that Orthodoxy would diminish the influence of the Conservative and Reform movements, not vice versa. His optimism made him a heroic figure in my eyes, and he remained such over many decades. I had much to do with him later in life, and he was of great help to me in numerous rabbinic matters. Every rabbi needs a hero to help guide him, and Rabbi Teitz played that role for me in many areas of Jewish public life.

My life and legal career in Chicago now underwent a major change that I never, even in my wildest nightmares, would have imagined. I received a phone call from a former yeshiva classmate of mine who was now an attorney. He represented another former classmate who had invested with me in an apartment building project. He accused me of fraud, demanded to see the books on the project, and was very aggressive. The investor's brother-in-law also called and threatened me with disbarment. I was devastated: How could my friends turn against me so viciously? Manny Finkel stiffened my backbone, forcing me to continue my Shabbat rabbinate, though my accuser prayed in that *minyan*.

Rumors quickly spread, sullying my reputation. Naturally, all my investors wanted out immediately. I liquidated everything I owned, including my home, and paid everyone back. Having been fairly wealthy, I was now considered a pauper, and a dishonest one at that. However, I slowly recovered my nerve and drive as my innocence became obvious publicly. I found another fine house, whose upkeep cost much less than that of our previous home, and we moved in.

The brother-in-law eventually apologized, as did his lawyer. The main party himself never did. He merely cashed the check compensating him for his investment. But he taught me a lesson: Never underestimate the destructive power of money.

Needless to say, this incident strained my family life. I was devastated by the pain my wife and parents felt because of this libel. Coupled with Jackie's life-threatening illness, this was a most difficult time for me. But somehow I persevered and righted the ship. Manny really helped save me from my troubles and depression through his unqualified friendship, resolve, and cleverness. I have always been in his debt for his invaluable assistance during this dark period of my life.

In November 1963, just after the assassination of President John F. Kennedy, I was sitting alone in the office of the tool and die company. It was right after the Thanksgiving party for my workers. (Everyone proclaimed the Empire kosher turkey far tastier than the usual fare. I never bothered to explain that it was the kashering salt that enhanced its flavor.) I looked up and saw my dear friend Rabbi Louis Aryeh Rottman at the door. Aryeh and I had spent many years together in yeshiva.

He was slightly older than I, and very close to Rabbi Kreiswirth. The latter – who had contacts all over the Jewish world – knew the Bendheim and Salomon families, who almost single-handedly supported a small Miami Beach congregation. Rabbi Kreiswirth recommended Aryeh to that congregation, and Aryeh, ever loyal to his beloved mentor and teacher, moved with his wife and children to Miami Beach and became the rabbi of that *shul*.

Rabbi Kreiswirth had plans for me too. He had left Chicago in 1955 to become the rabbi in Antwerp, but every time he returned to Chicago (approximately once a year) he met with me. Invariably, he would encourage me to leave law and business and become a rabbi. The Jewish world needed rabbinic leadership more than legal advice, he'd say. I always countered that I had to make a living, and my Shabbat rabbinate in Chicago paid nothing.

Now, all of a sudden, Aryeh Rottman appeared on my doorstep with a proposition. He said he had come as my friend but mainly as Rabbi Kreiswirth's agent. Aryeh had accepted a position in Long Beach, New York. He planned to open a yeshiva there, wildly hoping Rabbi Kreiswirth would leave Antwerp and serve as full-time head of the school. (That never happened.) In any event, Aryeh said he couldn't just desert his congregants in Miami Beach; he had to replace himself – with none other than me!

Rabbi Kreiswirth thought I was the man for the job, and Aryeh himself said he'd do everything possible to ensure my election as rabbi. I dismissed the idea as preposterous. But Rabbi Rottman is truly a righteous and holy Jew – and very persistent. He wouldn't leave my office until I'd promised at least to consider the position and, if invited by the congregation, to come to Miami Beach for a tryout. His tenacity wore me down, and I agreed.

When I came home and mentioned the incident to my wife, she wisely said nothing.

Months passed, and I heard nothing from Rabbi Rottman. I practically forgot about the matter, having settled back into my routine of law, business, learning, and teaching. (I taught a *Chumash* class Friday nights for teenage boys, and it was highly successful and gratifying). Thankful that my wife's health had been miraculously restored, I busied myself with my community work on behalf of Bais Yaakov Hebrew Parochial School and Telshe Yeshiva.

Then, two weeks before Shavuot 1964, Rabbi Rottman called.

Chapter 6

Challenge and Fulfillment in Miami Beach

"Now you'll finally be happy at what you're doing."

Rabbis Rottman and Kreiswirth worked assiduously for my election as rabbi of Congregation Beth Israel, pressuring me to take the selection process seriously. I had to dress and act "rabbinic," they implored me. But I had my own mind. I went to the tryout wearing a blue suit and a white straw hat.

Shavuot that year fell on Sunday, so I had a three-day audition, while my competitors – both experienced rabbis and worthy candidates – had only one Shabbat each. I conducted an all-night learning session on Shavuot, delivered sermons, taught Avot, Ruth, and Talmud, and generally had a good time. I arose early on Shabbat morning and walked the length of Collins Avenue, dazzled by the hotels, the colors, the warm breezes, and the semi-exotic nature of the city. For the first time in my life I ate a mango.

I enjoyed meeting the members of the small congregation. I sensed that many objected to Rabbi Rottman's imposing a rabbi on them, and everyone knew I was his candidate. Since I wasn't sure I would accept the position even if it were offered to me – though I was certainly intrigued by the congregation's potential – I wasn't very nervous. I was aware that Rabbi Rottman (together with Rabbi Alexander

Gross, head of the Greater Miami Hebrew Academy Day School, and Rabbi "Whitey" Horowitz, vice principal) had created a high school for boys – Mesivta of Greater Miami. If I became a rabbi in Miami Beach, I envisioned playing a role in that institution as well.

There were forty voting members in the congregation. Some spent most of the year in New York and New Jersey and only wintered in Miami Beach. Rabbi Rottman got their proxies to vote for me on their behalf. The resentment over Rabbi Rottman's meddling grew, and I ultimately won by only two votes – thanks to the proxies. It was all legal, but I felt I was starting off on the wrong foot. My wife and I discussed whether we should move to Miami Beach. For her, it meant leaving her brother and sister in Chicago and being far from her father in Detroit. For me, it meant leaving my parents for the first time in my life. The salary I was offered in Miami Beach was pretty measly – $9,000 a year plus a rent-free house that the synagogue owned. Some years I'd paid more than that in taxes alone.

But we decided to take the plunge. "Now you'll finally be happy at what you're doing," said Jackie, who knew me better than I knew myself, "and then the whole family will also be happy." I sold all my assets in Chicago, practically giving everything away to my partners and investors, and paid almost all of my debts. (I wasn't completely debt-free until three years later.) Then we packed the station wagon and drove off to our new life.

We arrived in the oppressive summer heat and humidity of Miami Beach in July 1964. We moved into a very small, three-bedroom house about six blocks from the synagogue – with no air conditioning. The children soon made friends and happily played outdoors all day. Jackie slipped seamlessly into the role of *rebbitzen*, and everyone immediately loved and appreciated her.

The congregation was bitterly divided because of the split vote electing me as rabbi, and I devoted my initial efforts to healing the breach. I reached out to those who had voted against me, and within a few months most had become my friends and supporters. However, the synagogue was flat broke (having just purchased Rabbi Rottman's house as a token severance payment to him) and could not cover my first paycheck, due August 1. So began my lifelong fundraising career.

I think most successful rabbis are also able fundraisers – the two professions are really one. Thanks to a few devoted synagogue officers, within a year the congregation was on firm financial footing, no longer dependent on one or two wealthy members who lived most of the year outside Florida. As finances improved, membership grew, the congregation expanded and was able to buy air conditioners for our home, and things were generally rosy.

My sermons improved too, and people walked sizable distances (to my chagrin, some even drove!) on Shabbat to hear what I had to say. Every day, I taught Mishnah, Talmud, and the weekly Torah reading. I arranged for women's groups and classes as well as for youth groups and children's activities. I spent quite a few hours a day in the tiny synagogue office, and made myself available to a wide variety of Jews who dropped in for advice, help, or conversation. Some just needed something to do, somewhere to go – and I was glad they chose to come to the *shul*. The little storefront congregation was full on Shabbat, and in the winter it was bursting at the seams. I was delighted with my job, and the synagogue became known as "Rabbi Wein's *Shul*."

The two teachers at the Mesivta of Greater Miami were both products of Telshe Yeshiva in Cleveland. As I had helped transplant the yeshiva to Chicago, I joined these teachers in trying to replicate that feat in Miami Beach. Rabbis Gross and Horowitz had taken over the Mesivta after Rabbi Rottman had left. For some arrogant reason, however, I thought I had inherited Rabbi Rottman's control of the high school, and clandestinely negotiated with Rabbi Mordechai Katz (head of Telshe Yeshiva in Cleveland) about sending a cadre of students to Miami Beach, as he had done in establishing the Chicago branch. Rabbis Gross and Horowitz were aghast at the plan and pointedly told me to forget it. But I persisted, enlisting a few congregants' support. At a public meeting held to discuss the idea, I realized that opposition was strong. Importing students would only split the small, still nascent community and indirectly cripple my standing as rabbi of the synagogue as well. Miami Beach was not Chicago. The plan was clearly premature, so I gave up on it. Now it was important to rebuild my bridges, especially with Rabbis Gross and Horowitz. I had overreached and suffered a well-deserved defeat. As the rabbis of the Talmud say, "He who overreaches,

reaches nothing." And I learned a significant lesson: Enthusiasm and self-confidence (and especially self-righteousness) must be tempered by a modicum of restraint and cool common sense. In retrospect, I freely admitted to Rabbi Gross and others that Telshe Yeshiva and Miami Beach in 1965 wouldn't have been a good match.

Many wealthy Jews from all over North America wintered in Miami Beach. In the pre-condo days, large kosher hotels accommodated these visitors. Several owners of these hotels were active members of my *shul*. They encouraged their guests to attend our synagogue, especially for Shabbat services. They touted me, the new young rabbi in town, as the main attraction. The winter visitors – many very important and well known in the Jewish world – flocked to the synagogue, as did newcomers to our neighborhood. Seating was rapidly becoming scarce.

Heaven helped Congregation Beth Israel. Our *shul* was located within a strip mall. On the corner was a large supermarket, part of an expanding chain owned by a wealthy Miami Beach Jew. The supermarket decided to purchase and demolish the entire strip in order to increase parking. After all the store owners had sold out to the supermarket, its lawyer invited the synagogue's officers to a meeting to finalize the purchase of our leasehold. In anticipation of this windfall, the congregation borrowed money and purchased a house and lot across the street, where we planned to move.

Our board of directors had appointed a committee of three to negotiate with the supermarket. For some reason, these three very accomplished businesspeople took me along to the meeting as well. The board had instructed them to demand the appraised value of our lease, which was $35,000 to $40,000. As we drove to the meeting, these experienced businessmen began discussing the negotiation. After a long deliberation, they agreed that $50,000 would be a windfall for the congregation.

At the meeting, the supermarket's lawyer was very curt and cold. He told us we were holding up a very important move for the supermarket and bluntly asked us, "How much do you want for your lease?" One committee member, searching for a starting point in the negotiation process, blurted out, "Seventy-five thousand dollars!" "Done!" said the lawyer without hesitation. "It's a deal."

On the way home, our committee members were crushed, thinking they should have asked for more. I tried consoling them, pointing out that we were more than willing to accept $50,000. But to no avail. "Rabbi," they said, "you don't understand how these money matters really work." I kept quiet, but I certainly had enough financial and human experience to understand how these money matters really do work.

We now had enough funds to build a new synagogue, and we hired a brilliant architect. Though non-Jewish, he captured the tone of our congregation and designed a building that was both striking and functional. Its roof was of draped concrete, recalling the curtained roof of the *Mishkan* in the desert. The sanctuary, round and beautiful, was surrounded with exquisite stained glass windows. The women's balcony was delicate and practical, with good sight lines. The building contained classrooms, a kitchen, a social hall, offices for the rabbi and the synagogue secretary, and a fine chapel/*beit midrash*, also decorated with impressive stained glass windows. Construction took fourteen months. I was on the job almost every day, supervising the process in addition to my usual rabbinic duties. I enjoyed the experience greatly.

Once the building was up, the synagogue was filled every Shabbat, and my extensive classes were also very well attended. I continued my

Dedicating the new synagogue building (Miami Beach, 1966)

daily Mishnah and Talmud classes and initiated a weekly Jewish history class for women. I felt I was really getting somewhere with the *shul*.

In our neighborhood there was no Conservative congregation, but there was a large Reform temple. Many Jews who were uncomfortable with Reform services drifted into our synagogue, though they were not Orthodox. Over time, they and their children became observant. It was *kiruv* before the term was yet known and popularized. As mentioned, some Jews drove to the *shul* to hear my Shabbat sermons. After what I thought was a reasonable time and they seemed closer to observance, I asked them to stop. Some actually moved into the neighborhood, while others found Shabbat apartments within walking distance of the synagogue. Still others ignored my request and kept driving. And others stopped coming altogether. I've always felt that the diversity and freedom of American Jewry defy easy solutions to its halachic problems or issues – at least as far as the pulpit rabbinate is concerned. And there is always another rabbi in the community poised to criticize whatever decision or policy the congregational rabbi makes. It has ever been this way in Jewish society.

Our children adjusted very well to Miami Beach and the Hebrew Academy. They all had friends, many less observant than we were. We always impressed upon our children that our family was special and that they should not be overly impressed or influenced by what their friends or classmates did or said. We didn't judge how others spoke, dressed, or behaved. We just established who we were as a family, allowed our children freedom, and relied on their good judgment, while laying down a code of behavior that they understood and adhered to pretty much ungrudgingly.

To enrich my son's Torah studies, I formed an after-school "hockey league" that met in the synagogue. After the boys played and had refreshments, I studied Mishnah and Talmud with them. I also conducted Shabbat afternoon Mishnah classes for the boys of the synagogue at my home, rewarding their attendance with candy. My wife conducted groups for the girls at the synagogue and presented an annual play that was a smash hit. ("The Brown Yarmulke" was named after "The Brown Derby," a play of that time.) Jackie was enormously talented and creative, and everyone loved her – something no rabbi can ever achieve.

These activities were a great boon to the education of the neighborhood children, and they were especially beneficial for our own kids. They were hardly deficient in their Jewish studies compared to their peers in larger Jewish communities and schools. Miami Beach provided our kids with a happy childhood as well as a very good education and a most acceptable social milieu. We sent the girls to camps in the Catskills for the summer, but our son went one year and didn't enjoy it at all.

The synagogue provided me with six weeks of summer vacation, and until the children were old enough to go to sleepaway camps, our family used this time to travel all over America, visiting relatives and taking in scenic sites and places of interest. I think my wife and I were more enthusiastic about these trips than our children, but in retrospect it was a good experience for all. Over the years, we visited all forty-eight states of the continental United States. Later in life, Jackie and I completed the mission by visiting Alaska and Hawaii as well.

Rabbi Gross, the principal of the Hebrew Academy, asked me to teach a *Chumash* class for half an hour a day to the seventh- and eighth-grade boys. The school couldn't pay me, yet I readily agreed, for by now (in my third year as a rabbi in Miami Beach) Rabbi Gross and I were not only colleagues but friends. All our children were close friends too. This half-hour class was enormously successful, and I have devoted friends and students today – almost a half century later – who became more observant as a result and later built their own generations of loyal and knowledgeable Jews. Some became leading rabbis and Torah scholars in America and Israel, while others undertook lay leadership of Jewish communities throughout the world.

As a lawyer and businessman, I had learned the skill of time management, multitasking without seeming harried. I even came home for lunch every day, and my wife and I treasured that time together. This was a far cry from my Chicago days, when I left home early in the morning and came back late at night. When our eight-year-old son was asked by one of the leading synagogue officers, "What do you want to be when you grow up?" Chaim immediately answered: "A rabbi." When the man asked why, Chaim quickly responded, "Because he never has to go to work." I was very busy, and my time was almost fully occupied, but Chaim was right – I never had to go to work.

For the first time, I had to issue *gittin* – Jewish divorces. The expert in this field was (and is) my friend from yeshiva, Rabbi David Lehrfield. He was kind enough to tutor me and guide me through the intricacies of the process. I also consulted regularly with my father-in-law, who was in charge of *gittin* in Detroit. I was always terribly nervous when I had to administer the granting of a *get*, often feeling sick afterward. Yet I became competent, and even sent *gittin* to women in Israel as well as in numerous communities in the United States and Canada. Through the necessary correspondence with rabbis in these far-flung communities, I came to know many of them.

As a rule, I attempted to send the couple to Rabbi Lehrfield, but many times that option was simply unavailable; as the local rabbi, I had to shoulder the responsibility. I once even reconciled a couple seeking a divorce. Generally, though, divorce proceedings weren't something I enjoyed. But like many rabbinic tasks – such as delivering a eulogy or unveiling a cemetery monument – it was a duty one could not ignore. Later, when I moved to Monsey, New York, I never participated in administering *gittin*, since the established local rabbinical courts handled them. And in Jerusalem, I had nothing more to do with these proceedings either, though I sometimes advised the court when I knew the couple and their circumstances.

Aside from these cases, I enjoyed interacting with my community. Many of my congregants were truly fascinating. One was a ninety-six-year-old, Lithuanian-born Jew who was alert, clever, and very wealthy. I always visited him when raising funds for the Mesivta. One Purim, I brought him *mishloach manot* and stayed to chat. "Do you want to know why I've lived such a long life?" he suddenly asked. Before I could answer, he continued: "I was an orphan in Kovno [Kaunas, Lithuania] when I was ten or eleven years old. I was living on the street near the *Mussar* house [a center for the study of Jewish ethics]. The holy men there took me in, bathed and fed me, taught me, and looked after me for four years. One year, after the *Neilah* prayer on Yom Kippur, the group danced before beginning the *Maariv* services."

Then he sang me the melody to which they danced eighty-five years ago!

"I was dancing with them, and I held the hand of Rabbi Yitzchak (Itzele) Blazer (Peterburger), the famous disciple of Rabbi Yisrael Lipkin of Salant. I was only a child, so when I danced I was a little wild with my feet. I kicked Rabbi Blazer in the shin! Rabbi Blazer took my face in his hands and said to me, 'My dear boy, may you live a long life, but please don't kick anyone in the shin again.' So you see, Rabbi Blazer blessed me with a long life. And here I am – still alive!"

He lived another two years, never losing any of his faculties, and passed away peacefully. Shaking the hand that had held Rabbi Yitzchak Blazer's was a memorable moment for me.

The tense days prior to the Six-Day War of 1967 were stressful for Jews the world over, and certainly in Miami Beach. The obvious reluctance of the world powers to counteract the Arab threat to annihilate Israel raised the specter of a second Holocaust. Additional prayer services were held in my synagogue, and many people seeking hope and comfort amid their dread came to the *shul* just to sit there for much of the day.

The Jewish community reached out to the local churches, asking them to petition the US government to intervene on Israel's behalf. One pastor I visited was very cold to me, refusing to get involved or countenance any of my requests. I sensed that he resented having so many Jewish residents in the neighborhood. He probably was saddened by the Israeli victory a week later.

Of course, for us the impact of that miraculous war was enormous. I was driving when the radio broadcast the news about the Israeli triumph in Jerusalem and the return of the Western Wall to Jewish hands. I stopped my car, tears streaming down my cheeks, and saw that many other drivers had also stopped. Jews were hugging each other and dancing in the street. That first Shabbat after the war, the synagogue was packed, and it was a joyous service.

My meeting with the pastor was one of two encounters with Christian clergy. A few days after our new synagogue building was featured in a local newspaper, I received a call from a nun, the principal of a Catholic girls' school. She asked if the older classes could tour the building. "After all," she mused, "our savior must have prayed in such an Orthodox synagogue." I could hardly refuse her request. Sure enough, one day about forty seventh- and eighth-grade girls showed up with the principal, expecting a guided tour of our premises and an explanation of Judaism and the synagogue – in an hour. Somehow I did it.

The nun then asked me if they could pray in the synagogue. I asked what prayers she had in mind, and she assured me that they would only recite three psalms of David. They had brought their Psalters along for the occasion. I asked to see one. At the end of every psalm, in the same font as the psalm itself, was a direct reference to the Trinity. I told the nun that she and her students could recite the psalm itself, but not the concluding sentence. She looked at me in wonderment. "But why not? Is it not part of the psalm?" I told her that indeed it wasn't, and as proof I showed her a Soncino English translation of Psalms. Her response was quite revealing: "I never understood why you Jews stubbornly refused to accept Christianity, since your own King David in Psalms expressly endorsed the Trinity. Now I'm beginning to understand." She visited the synagogue with her students some years later as well. That was pretty much the extent of my interfaith activities in Miami Beach.

Except for my unexpected radio performance. At the time, there was a struggling talk show host on local radio by the name of Larry King. Via a mutual friend, a member of my congregation communicated to King that I would make a great guest on his show. He invited me to come on the show on the deadest radio night of the year – December 24. We spent an hour discussing what rabbis, and Jews in general, thought about Christianity. This topic came at me without warning, so I had to think fast. With the extraordinary Divine protection that accompanies such circumstances, I didn't say anything too stupid, too accommodating, or too controversial. When I returned home, my wife (one of the few listeners that night) complimented my performance. No one else did, but I enjoyed the experience.

I was a guest on Larry King's show quite a few times after that. He was a great interviewer even then, and I was fascinated by broadcasting. I have since been interviewed a number of times on television and radio in both the United States and Israel. I always find it exciting and challenging. It's remarkable that one's words may influence countless people completely unknown to him.

But my primary interest was in providing for my community,

both spiritually and physically. The young rabbis in the Miami area had organized a Council of Orthodox Rabbis. We tried to set up acceptable *kashrut* standards in order to provide the basic stores necessary for an observant community – a bakery and a butcher shop. We found it difficult to find Sabbath-observant Jews to own and operate such stores. But we devised inspection systems and schedules to safeguard the *kashrut* of these two fledgling enterprises. There was many a hiccup along the way.

Before coming to Florida, when I learned I would be the rabbi of Congregation Beth Israel, I spent several weeks in the back of a kosher butcher shop owned by a former yeshiva classmate of mine in Chicago. So I had practical experience regarding the deveining of blood vessels and the removal of non-kosher fat in the forequarters of beef. Now that I was in Miami Beach, this knowledge was put to the test.

For our local butcher shop, all the meat was to be imported from a well-known Hasidic wholesaler in Brooklyn. He would ship meat to Miami completely *kashered*, so our butcher would only have to cut and package the final product. On one of my regular visits to the meat cooler, I noticed a number of forequarters that hadn't been deveined, and from which the non-kosher fat hadn't been removed. Since the meat had already been soaked and salted, there was no way to salvage it for the kosher market. I called the Brooklyn wholesaler and told him that somehow a mistake had been made. He answered me derisively: "I thought that you Litvaks didn't care about such matters." I informed him that he would never again sell meat in Miami Beach to the hotels whose *kashrut* was certified by the OU (the Union of Orthodox Congregations of the United States and Canada, better known as the Orthodox Union), and certainly not to this butcher shop. I kept my promise as long as I was in Miami Beach.

It was quite a lesson: Never be fooled by beards or long, black coats when money is involved. The next, extremely painful incident proves this point once again.

My friend and predecessor in Miami Beach, Rabbi Rottman, left his rabbinic position in Long Beach and moved to Jerusalem, there to found and head Yeshivat Mercaz HaTorah in the Talpiot neighborhood. His yeshiva was popular and successful, mainly due to his holy character, great sensitivity, and loving care for his students. He naturally consulted with Rabbi Kreiswirth in Antwerp on the move, and insisted on listing him on the yeshiva stationery as its *rosh yeshiva*, though Rabbi Kreiswirth was hardly a permanent force or presence there.

An old hotel building had been bought for the yeshiva, and Rabbi Rottman was raising funds to refurbish and expand it. He formed an American charity – American Friends of Yeshivat Mercaz HaTorah – and I became the treasurer and a signatory on its bank account. As such, the bank that held the account was in Miami Beach. I deposited the American checks that Rabbi Rottman obtained on his numerous fundraising forays in the United States. I also periodically gave him signed checks that he would convert into Israeli currency to pay the yeshiva staff. One day, I received a call from the bank manager. There were three checks, each for $100,000, drawn on the American Friends account. These checks had been cashed at an Israeli bank, which was now demanding that the American bank make good on them.

Sick to my stomach, I called Rabbi Rottman in Jerusalem and pieced the story together bit by bitter bit. It seems that a charlatan – with a long, black coat and a long beard – had befriended Rabbi Rottman and offered to help him get a good exchange rate for his American checks. The rabbi trusted him, and for six months everything was in order. Then the thief came to Rabbi Rottman and asked for three blank checks, because he could make a special deal that would profit the yeshiva. The rabbi naively complied. In cahoots with a crooked bank manager in Israel, the swindler had cashed the checks for $300,000.

Desperately seeking guidance, I called Rabbi Kreiswirth. He told me, "The yeshiva belongs to Rabbi Rottman. Do whatever he wants." Despite threats of bodily harm by thugs in long, black coats and beards, Rabbi Rottman went to the Israeli police with the story. The bank manager was finally arrested and confessed to the scam. He served time in prison, but his partner fled to America and established himself as a holy man in Boro Park.

The Israeli bank was insured against such occurrences, so the Miami bank was compensated, and I could get back to normal life – after six harrowing weeks of tension and fury.

(Thirty-five years later, I met the thief – at an engagement party in Monsey. I identified myself, reminded him of the incident, and told him that even though I could no longer take legal action against him, I would never forgive him, because he showed no remorse. He blanched momentarily but soon resumed his holy man persona, bestowing his blessings on all those foolish enough to ask for them. His ever-present cohort collected a fee from each one and piously proclaimed that the money would be used for "charitable purposes.")

I withdrew my name from the American Friends account, though I continued helping Rabbi Rottman and the yeshiva however I could. I consider it a privilege to have been Rabbi Rottman's friend for over six decades.

Chapter 7

In the Right Place at the Right Time

"I grasped the greatness and diversity of the Jewish People."

One of the most significant blessings of being a rabbi in Miami Beach was that many of the foremost leaders of the Jewish People passed through to escape the cold northern winter and raise funds for their institutions. I had the privilege of knowing truly great people simply by being in the right place at the right time, i.e., Miami Beach in the 1960s and early 1970s. I was a young American rabbi, beardless, and fairly acculturated, yet some of the most extraordinary people befriended and inspired me. Among them were: Rabbi Yosef Shlomo Kahaneman, the Ponivezher Rav, and his son, Avraham; Rabbi Yoel Teitelbaum, the Satmar Rebbe; Rabbi Mordechai Shulman, *rosh yeshiva* of the Slabodka Yeshiva in Bnei Brak; Rabbi Avraham Yehoshua Heschel, the Kapischnitzer Rebbe of Brooklyn; Rabbi Meir Grunwald, the Teitcher Rav of Toronto; Rabbi Shneur Kotler, *rosh yeshiva* of Beth Medrash Govoha in Lakewood, New Jersey; Rabbi Yaakov Kamenetsky, *rosh yeshiva* of Mesivta Torah Vodaath, Brooklyn; Rabbi Henoch Leibowits, *rosh yeshiva* of the Rabbinical Seminary of America/Chafetz Chaim; Rabbi Joseph B. Soloveitchik, *rosh yeshiva* of Rabbi Isaac Elchanan Theological Seminary (RIETS), Yeshiva University; Rabbi Shlomo Goren, then chief rabbi

Parlor meeting on behalf of Ponivezh Yeshiva at my home in Miami Beach.
Seated, right to left: Rabbis Leizer Levin, Y. Gruenwald, and Yosef Shlomo
Kahaneman; standing, right to left: R. C. Rosenzweig, Mr. Leo Rappaport,
R. Mordechai Shulman, me, and Mr. Maurice Goldring

of the Israel Defense Forces and later Ashkenazic chief rabbi of Israel;
Rabbi Immanuel Jakobovits, rabbi of the Fifth Avenue Synagogue, New
York, and later chief rabbi of Great Britain; Rabbi Leo Jung, rabbi of the
Jewish Center of Manhattan; Rabbi Norman Lamm, then associate rabbi
of the Jewish Center of Manhattan and later president of Yeshiva Univer-
sity; Rabbi Emmanuel Gettinger, rabbi of the Young Israel of the West
Side, and a future *mechutan* of mine; Rabbi Pinchas M. Teitz, leader of
the Orthodox community in Elizabeth, New Jersey; Rabbi Alexander
Rosenberg, rabbi in Yonkers, New York, and rabbinic administrator of
the OU Kashrut Division; Rabbi Samson Raphael Weiss, executive vice
president of the OU; Rabbi Naftali Zvi Yehuda Riff, rabbi in Camden and
Cherry Hill, New Jersey; Rabbi Moshe Feinstein, *rosh yeshiva* of Mesivta
Tiferes Yerushalayim, New York; Rabbi Eliyahu Kitov (Monkotofsky),
famed educator and author from Jerusalem; Rabbi Aaron Paperman,
executive vice president of Telshe Yeshiva, Cleveland; Rabbi Naftali
Neuberger, executive vice president, Ner Israel Rabbinical College,
Baltimore; David Pardo, founder and head of Ohr Hachaim Girls'

Institutions, Bnei Brak; Rabbi Nissan Tukachinsky, head of Yeshivat Etz Chaim and the United Charity Institutions, both of Jerusalem; Rabbi David Lifshitz, *rosh yeshiva* at Rabbi Isaac Elchanan Theological Seminary and president of Ezras Torah; Rabbi Yitzchak David Grossman, rabbi of Migdal Ha'emek and founder of the Migdal Ohr Institutions in Israel (who was very young when I met him); Rabbi Moshe Sherer, executive head and later president of Agudath Israel of America; Dr. Yosef Burg, Israeli government minister and leading religious Zionist; Shmuel Shaulson, vice mayor of Jerusalem; Rabbi Eliezer Silver, rabbi in Cincinnati and dean of the American Orthodox rabbinate; Elie Wiesel, famed Holocaust memoirist and Nobel Prize winner; Major Maurice Jaffee, founder and executive head of the Great Synagogue of Jerusalem; Rabbi Yehoshua Huttner, executive head of Yad HaRav Herzog and the *Encyclopedia Talmudit* project, Jerusalem; Rabbi Alexander Linchner, son-in-law of Rabbi Shraga Feivel Mendelowitz and founder and head of Boys Town, Jerusalem; Menachem Porush, Knesset member and leader of Agudath Israel in Israel.

I also became lifelong friends with Rabbi Emanuel Feldman, then of Atlanta. And I met such Israeli leaders as Yitzchak Rabin and Yigal Alon. This list is incomplete, but you can readily assess how fortunate I was to come into contact with all these notables. Through knowing them, I grasped the greatness and diversity of the Jewish People.

Many of these people were guests in our home. It was most stimulating to converse with them. They also expanded my Jewish knowledge, and through many of them I glimpsed the world of European Jewry that was and would never be again. They gave me an insider's perspective on the development of the nascent State of Israel. I have inspiring recollections of each of these men.

Rabbi Kahaneman, the Ponivezher Rav, enlisted me to be his driver a few mornings a week as he raised funds for his yeshiva. Just being in his company was an honor and a joy. I learned a great deal from him about people, life, fundraising, and – above all – Torah knowledge and values. He loved all Jews (no easy task), and they loved him back. He taught me that one must accept personal insults and slights for the sake of Torah. I witnessed many "miraculous" feats of fundraising. He could get money from a stone.

During those years, I knew a wonderful man in my congregation. He was a widower without children, though he had nephews and nieces. He was quite wealthy, but at only fifty-five had suffered two heart attacks and survived cancer. His doctors advised him to live out his few remaining years in the Florida sunshine rather than the frost and snow of northern New Jersey. So he retired to Miami Beach, where he became a leader in our community. Mindful of his physicians' predictions, he dutifully purchased an annuity plan that would provide him with a generous income until age ninety. He fully expected to die before then.

But the Lord thought otherwise, and this fellow reached his ninetieth birthday fully well, still productive, and active. But now he had no income, and he rapidly used up his savings. No bank would advance him a mortgage due to his age. So I organized deliveries of food and other necessities to him.

The man had been a staunch supporter of the Ponivezh Yeshiva, giving Rav Kahaneman a sizable donation every year. One day, the Rav instructed me to take him to this man's house. I told him that his former supporter had no money now and that our visit under these circumstances would embarrass him. Nevertheless, the Rav insisted. We arrived and sat down in the man's living room. The Rav announced in his mellifluous voice, and with that wonderful smile on his face, "Until now, you have generously helped the yeshiva in its times of need. Now the yeshiva is going to repay you in kind. Every month the yeshiva will send you the amount of your monthly annuity check, and I want you to continue living as you always have." Offsetting the man's protests, he added, "After a hundred and twenty years, you and I will straighten out this matter between us." As we left the bewildered old gentleman, the Rav told me, "A yeshiva is also obligated to perform acts of kindness and mercy to others." And that is exactly what he did. For the next four years, until the man passed away, the yeshiva sent him a monthly check. Upon his death, he left his house in Miami Beach to the yeshiva.

On another occasion, Rabbi Kahaneman explained to me how the Jewish People had somehow recovered, and even prospered, after the terrible events of the Holocaust. "A child, God forbid, falls ill with a dreaded disease and is near death. And then, miraculously, he rallies and survives and can return home to continue recuperating. Initially, the child's parents will grant his every wish – toys, pizza, ice cream, anything. It's the same with us. After surviving the Holocaust, God (so to speak) granted our wishes – a state of our own in the Land of Israel, the revival of Torah study and yeshivot, large families, political influence, unimagined personal and national prosperity, and all the other blessings we now enjoy. But eventually there will be a return to normalcy, and we must be prepared for that." No one was more optimistic about the future of the Jewish People and Torah study than he. Yet no one was more realistic about the problems we faced us as a nation and as observant Jews.

Rabbi Kahaneman once told me that on Israel Independence Day the Israeli flag flies over his yeshiva in Bnei Brak. When visitors protested that practice, he responded, "In Lithuania, on Lithuanian Independence Day, I flew the Lithuanian flag from the roof of the yeshiva in Ponivezh. My friends, it is no worse here!" He cleverly told me that on Independence Day he follows "the custom of David Ben-Gurion" regarding prayer: no *Hallel* and no *Tachanun*. He recalled the following conversation with the Israeli prime minister: "'We have a strong army,' the prime minister told me. 'We have *bitachón* [with the modern emphasis on the last syllable].' I answered him, 'I have *bitáchon* [using the traditional Ashkenazic emphasis].' He asked me, 'What's the difference?' and I replied, 'One is *milra* and the other *mil'el*!'"[1]

Rabbi Kahaneman once asked me to organize a meeting of young couples at my home, because he wanted to address them. I told him I didn't think the meeting would be successful, since young people don't have large sums to donate to charity. He smiled and said, "Please do as I ask." I complied, and the following week my wife and I hosted about twenty couples. The Rav spoke to them informally but powerfully. The gist of what he said was this: 'One and a half million Jewish children were killed in the Holocaust. The souls of those children are floating above us, searching for a body. Please give them bodies." I was astounded by the request, and by the way it was phrased. The next year, a bumper crop of babies was born in our congregation. What a great man!

---

1. *Milra* and *mil'el* are Aramaic terms referring to emphasis on the last or previous syllable, respectively. In Hebrew, however, *ra* means bad, while *el* means supreme.

We became very close. He even offered me the executive vice presidency of the yeshiva. He promised to build me a villa in Bnei Brak. I saw the disappointment on his face when I declined. Years later, the Rav's son, Rabbi Avraham Kahaneman, told me it would have been a boon for the yeshiva had I accepted the offer, but it would have been less than pleasant for me in the turbulent milieu of the yeshiva and of Bnei Brak. He also told me that when his father passed away, the yeshiva was $5 million in debt due to its expansion in Bnei Brak and its branches in Ashdod and in the Galilee. Yet just five years after his father's death, this enormous debt had been paid off. Incredulous, I asked how he had accomplished that feat. He answered: "When my father was alive, he was the one who worked, and I helped him. Now I'm working and he's helping me."

When we came to Israel, my wife and I joined Rav Kahaneman and his wife for Shabbat lunch. I felt so blessed and fortunate to have become a life student of his. Wisdom, faith, great Torah knowledge, holiness, and unbounded energy and optimism were all wrapped up in this great person. I never again met his equal as a visionary and builder of Torah and the Jewish People. When he established the Ponivezh cemetery in Bnei Brak, he told me, "During my lifetime I raised funds for the yeshiva. Since I'll be buried in this cemetery, people will pay a large premium to be buried here too. Even when I'm dead, I'll be raising funds for the yeshiva!" And so it is.[2]

A number of my congregants were followers of the Satmar Rebbe, Rabbi Yoel Teitelbaum. They didn't necessarily subscribe to his views on modernity or the State of Israel, but because of their family traditions and pre-war connections to Romania/Hungary, to Szighet and Satmar, they remained respectful of and helpful to him. One of these congregants lived in a waterfront mansion within walking distance of my synagogue. When the Rebbe came to Miami Beach for two months during the winter, the mansion was turned over to him for his exclusive use. Hundreds of the Rebbe's followers accompanied him on this sojourn, and many

---

2. In fact, my father-in-law, Rabbi Leizer Levin, is buried there along with many other distinguished rabbis.

found accommodations in my neighborhood. Initially, they prayed in my synagogue, but I realized immediately that these Hasidim and my usual congregants were not a good match. So I gave the guests the chapel room, while we regulars used the main sanctuary. Rabbi Nissan Tukachinsky, who was visiting Miami Beach on behalf of Yeshivat Etz Chaim, deemed this arrangement "a stroke of genius." The Satmar followers were very appreciative of this gesture too, informing the Rebbe of it.

For some reason, the Rebbe really took a liking to me. His followers couldn't fathom what he saw in an unbearded young American rabbi of a fairly modern congregation. But if the Rebbe liked and accepted me, they had to as well. Actually, the Rebbe did me a great favor immediately upon arrival in Miami Beach. When we constructed our new synagogue, I insisted that a *mikvah* be included on the premises. With the help of several well-known rabbinical experts, the facility was built and functioned well. All fees generated by the synagogue's *mikvah* were turned over to the community *mikvah*, in South Beach. Nevertheless, some questioned the validity of the structure and asked pointedly, "Who is Wein to build a *mikvah*?" I ignored these mean-spirited people, for I knew I could never convince them of the error of their ways. The entire matter was laid to rest when the Satmar Rebbe came to town and immersed daily in the synagogue *mikvah*. He later complimented me on its splendid construction, both halachically and physically.

Naturally, I paid a formal visit to Rabbi Teitelbaum. I was pleasantly surprised when he visited my home in return. We had long talks about Torah, the rabbinate, and Jewish life, though I studiously avoided talking to him about the State of Israel. He gave me some solid rabbinic advice: Study up on what to do when a potential mistake is found in a *sefer Torah*. That way, one can solve the problem quickly, decisively, and correctly. As a young rabbi he had been tripped up by such a situation and resolved never to be caught that way again. And his advice came in handy for me too, almost immediately.

The Rebbe encouraged the young men of his community to marry early. He told me he was once asked what to do when a groom and a *bar mitzvah* boy were both in the synagogue on Shabbat: Who took precedence for *Maftir*? He answered, "Whoever is older!"

He had a marvelous sense of humor.

I was very active in the Miami Beach Mesivta, voluntarily teaching the eleventh-grade Talmud class daily. I invited many of the luminaries visiting Miami Beach in the winter to address the thirty boys in our school. I felt it was important for the young men's education that they see and hear these extraordinary individuals. Of course, I invited Rabbi Teitelbaum to speak as well. He said it was a good thing Miami Beach had such a yeshiva. He then asked me, "Does the school conduct secular studies daily on its own premises?" When I answered in the affirmative, he told me the following anecdote: "A man walked into a restaurant and ordered soup. Upon receiving it, he peered into the bowl and saw dead flies floating in the liquid. He called over the waiter and asked, 'If it's all the same to you, may I have the soup and the flies separately?'" I understood his point. He never spoke at the school. But he never told me to discontinue its secular studies either.

The Rebbe was well aware of his followers' imperfections, such as speaking Hungarian as though it were some sort of holy tongue. He told me his rabbinical court supervised a certain butcher shop in the Williamsburg neighborhood of New York, where the Satmar Hasidim resided. But the butcher soon complained that they wouldn't buy from him. The Rebbe checked into the matter and found that they didn't trust the butcher's *kashrut* since he couldn't speak Hungarian!

Rabbi Teitelbaum had great love and compassion for his Hasidim, many of whom were Holocaust survivors. He admired their faith in God and Judaism despite their terrible ordeal. When children requested his blessing, he would instruct them to go over to Jews with numbers tattooed on their arms and receive blessings from *them*.

The Rebbe looked out for the economic and social welfare of his people. He told me Satmar's foray into the kosher food industry was fueled not so much by higher standards as by the necessity to strengthen the community financially. He demanded that those who were not of a scholarly bent earn a living. He established a network of institutions of self-help, charity, and kindness – and all Jews were precious in his eyes. Satmar helped any Jew in need.

The Rebbe's face shone with an inner light. He didn't go to bed, but rather dozed off for a few moments, even in mid-conversation. He would rapidly awaken and continue where the conversation had left off. My wife was very friendly with the wives of both the Ponivezher Rav and Rabbi Teitelbaum; she often helped organize women's teas for them, as well as taking them shopping and to other "women's activities."

As you can see, the Miami Beach experience was a wondrous one for the Wein family.

While still a student in Rabbi Kreiswirth's class in Chicago, I heard a lecture by Rabbi Eliyahu Kitov that made a deep impression on me. When I met up with him in Miami Beach a decade later, I reminded him of that speech. I used his classic work *Ish U'Veito* in its English translation (*A Jew and His Home*) as the basis of a class for the young couples in our synagogue.

Rabbi Kitov was a brilliant, fiery personality. And he viewed daily events differently from most of us. He saw everything through a Tanachic lens. Rabbi Alexander Gross once drove him to the airport to catch his return flight to Israel. After issuing his boarding pass, the woman at the ticket counter wished him a safe and pleasant flight. Rabbi Kitov responded in a booming voice, "Amen!" As everyone stared at him, he turned to Rabbi Gross and explained, "Our matriarch Sarah is told by someone she assumes is an Arab that she'll bear a child within the year. Sarah laughs at this unlikely prediction by this unlikely person. The Lord reprimands her in His conversation with Avraham, asking, 'Why did Sarah laugh at such good tidings?'" Rabbi Kitov interpreted this criticism to mean she should have said, "Amen!" Whenever anyone wishes you well, he asserted, your response should be, "Amen!"

I later met Rabbi Kitov's daughter, Naama Nothman, a famous painter in Johannesburg. She told me her father had encouraged her to develop her artistic talent and even sent her to Paris to study.

A man of great knowledge and breadth, Rabbi Kitov was, in my opinion, much underappreciated.

Rabbi Alexander Rosenberg, rabbinic administrator of the ou Kashrut Division, visited Miami Beach regularly during the winter. As mentioned, some of the kosher hotels there were owned and operated by my congregants. Rabbi Rosenberg asked me to be the ou supervising rabbi of these hotels. I told him I was concerned about conflicting interests:

I was the rabbi and confidant of these hotel owners, but as the enforcer of OU standards, I might seem overly strict and cause them considerable expense. He gave me his gentle, enigmatic smile and simply answered, "Well, I'm interested in seeing how you'll handle the situation."

I spent a good deal of time with Rabbi Rosenberg during his visits and learned a lot, especially regarding practical *kashrut* matters and judging people. He confided in me the inner workings of the OU and its personnel as well as his opinions about other Jewish matters. He was clever, insightful, straight, scholarly, astute, and altruistic to a fault. Even when he wasn't in Miami Beach, we spoke regularly by phone. His insights on rabbis, laymen, and synagogue life were quite instructive. The bond of deep affection between us transcended the ordinary relationship of a *kashrut* supervisor and a rabbinic administrator.

Rabbi Rosenberg was a masterful negotiator and a most commanding and distinguished figure. After World War II, he spent a number of years in the DP camps in Europe, providing kosher food and assisting survivors physically and spiritually. His greatest pleasure was to stand on a street corner in Williamsburg during *Chol Hamoed* and watch their children playing and laughing in their holiday finery. He helped many survivors establish themselves in the kosher food industry, granting them OU supervision and accreditation for next to nothing. Some within the OU's lay Kashrut Commission objected that the OU wasn't a charitable organization, but Rabbi Rosenberg was unfazed. "A rabbi needs only one strong supporter in his congregation or organization," he explained to me, "someone who will stand behind him even if he doesn't necessarily agree with the rabbi's stance on a particular issue. The chairman of the OU Kashrut Commission, Nathan K. Gross, is such a person. He always backs my decisions. So nothing else really matters."

My greatest difficulty in supervising the kosher hotels was Pesach. Rabbi Rosenberg's policy was not to grant an OU approval for Pesach programs held in venues that were non-kosher the rest of the year. I know this policy sounds anachronistic now, but it had great merit: The kitchen and dining room staffs of the year-round kosher hotels were already trained and disciplined in matters of *kashrut*. The chefs and maître d's were aware that no deviations would be tolerated and that their jobs depended upon upholding the *kashrut* standards. The chef knew that if he ran short on a certain ingredient, he couldn't just run out to a grocery store and purchase it. In contrast, the staff at venues that were non-kosher all year round had no such training, discipline, or mindset. The days before Pesach were harrowing for me and for the kitchen staffs as well. I was always satisfied, however, that the food was strictly kosher for Pesach.

Since I was in charge of selling *chametz* in these hotels, I asked Rabbi Rosenberg whether to refuse the usual gratuity given to rabbis for this service. I originally intended never to accept money for rabbinical services, but Rabbi Kreiswirth dissuaded me, "You cannot ruin it for the synagogue's next rabbi," he said. "Gratuities are traditionally given to rabbis for their services, and it's kosher money." Rabbi Rosenberg, however, gave me a Solomonic answer: "Never take money from these hotels – but you can take home Pesach desserts. Your wife will appreciate it, and a rabbi's main task is to keep his wife happy."

Just as I had an easy ride in Miami Beach with my wonderful congregation, my *kashrut* supervision of the ou hotels went relatively smoothly. The owners and their families, all observant Jews and many of them members of my congregation, became our friends, and I taught their children in the synagogue, Hebrew Academy, and Mesivta. They never took advantage of our relationship to deviate from ou *kashrut* standards or policies.

Through my regular visits to these kosher hotels, I met more of the leading rabbis and lay leaders in the Jewish world. I was often invited to speak at affairs in the hotels, and people beyond Miami Beach began noticing me. My synagogue sponsored a lecture series that featured Rabbis Norman Lamm and Emmanuel Gettinger. Rabbi Lamm felt I had talent and ability, and advised me to write articles and even books. I took him seriously and wrote a short monograph about the Vilna Gaon, which I distributed to my congregants. I also contributed articles to both *The Jewish Observer* (published by Agudath Israel) and *Jewish Life* (later *Jewish Action*, the magazine of the Orthodox Union). Saul Bernstein, ou publications editor, also visited Miami Beach and encouraged my efforts.

However, my main focus – aside from my duties at my synagogue, the Mesivta, and the Hebrew Academy – was on writing a doctoral thesis in Hebrew on the subject of *ger toshav*, a special type of convert to Judaism who lives in the Land of Israel but need not observe all the Torah's commandments. I once complained to my mentor and teacher, Rabbi Kreiswirth, that I had no one with whom to learn Torah regularly in Miami Beach. "Writing is the best study partner," he replied. He also told me that successful writing requires much erasing.

During summer vacations, when our family found itself in Chicago visiting relatives, I studied at the Hebrew Theological College in Skokie. Rabbi Dr. Leonard Mishkin taught history, Dr. Joseph Babad taught Midrash, and Dr. Eliezer Berkovits taught philosophy. I gained a great deal from these courses, which expanded my horizons of Jewish thought and life, and I became close to these masterful teachers.

My thesis blossomed into a short book, *Chikrei Halachah*, published by Mossad HaRav Kook. I did a tremendous amount of research and very intensive and satisfying study in writing this work. Rabbi Kreiswirth wrote a letter of approbation for it, and he was absolutely right – writing proved to be my best study partner.

As Jews from all over the world visited and attended my synagogue in Miami Beach, I was, after a number of years, offered rabbinic positions in Australia, South Africa, England, New York, Montreal, Toronto, and elsewhere. My family and I were quite happy in Miami Beach, so I never really considered relocating. However, when a synagogue in Queens asked me to apply, Rabbi Kreiswirth recommended that I do so. My wife and I were unhappy with how the synagogue treated us (we were housed in a nursing home during our stay!), and I told the place I wasn't interested. Nevertheless, my candidacy continued to be pushed. Fortunately, I wasn't chosen. Though I interviewed for other rabbinic positions thereafter, I wasn't serious about leaving Miami Beach. This was especially true after I visited Israel, for the first time accompanied by Jackie, in late 1967. We decided that if we were moving, it should be to Israel. While there, my wife and I became acquainted with wonderful relatives from both our families – such as my uncle, the distinguished Rabbi Tuvia Wein of Rechovot, who attended my son's *bar mitzvah* in Miami Beach – and they remained influential in our lives.

When we visited Israel again in 1968, we were so overcome emotionally that we purchased an apartment being built in Jerusalem's Bayit Vegan neighborhood. The price was $40,000, which we didn't have. The contractor was a well-known religious Jew (and later a Knesset member) who was starting out in construction. A close friend had recommended him. We bought the apartment based on plans shown to us, and trusted the contractor to live up to his promises. A member of my synagogue in Miami Beach was kind enough to obtain a loan for me from a local bank for the entire $40,000, which I paid the contractor in advance. My wife began teaching regularly at the Hebrew Academy, and her whole paycheck went to paying back the loan. We eventually discharged it over the next six years.

The apartment ultimately bore little resemblance to the plans. In addition, the contractor had built two illegal apartments in the building, which he now was attempting to legalize in city hall amid great controversy. As a final blow, he had mortgaged the entire building to an Israeli bank and never delivered any legal title to us for our apartment. All my conversations and pleading with him were for naught.

My old friend Manny Finkel and his family moved to Israel in 1973 and became a member of the Israeli bar. Manny sued the contractor on my behalf, and the judge ordered him to put the apartment in our name free and clear of any encumbrances within ninety days, or face a heavy fine and possible jail time for fraud. Needless to say, this court order concentrated the contractor's mind wonderfully. It enabled him somehow to solve his "problems" regarding our apartment, and the place was finally put in our name, and all the liens against it removed.

But we had lost all desire to live there. We rented out the apartment, and my son and his family lived in it for several years during his yeshiva/*kollel* studies in Israel.

Among our tenants were Rabbi Aaron Paperman and his wife, close friends from Miami Beach. Rabbi Paperman was a great storyteller. My favorite story of his was about his stint in Italy as the Jewish chaplain in the American Fifth Army during World War II. As Pesach approached, Rabbi Paperman was most concerned that the matzos from the Jewish Welfare Board in the United States had not yet arrived. He appealed to General Mark Clark, commander of the Fifth Army, to expedite the shipment. Clark referred the request to the quartermaster general, a jovial Italian American. He immediately took matters in hand, and on his own volition, baked five tons of matzos according to his own special recipe. Rabbi Paperman was horrified and in a major quandary. Fortunately, the Board's matzos arrived two weeks before Pesach. Rabbi Paperman conducted a *Seder* for five thousand Jewish troops in Rome's main train station. The *Seder* was attended by General Clark and the quartermaster general. As the latter munched on the imported matzo, he loudly exclaimed, "Mine are tastier!"

We eventually sold the apartment in Bayit Vegan at a considerable profit and used the money to purchase a flat in a building Manny Finkel was constructing in the Rechavia neighborhood of Jerusalem. This time, everything was built according to specifications, without any aggravation. And my friend Manny sold it to us at a bargain price. Sometimes friendship overrides even money.

After his Bar Mitzvah, we sent our son to Telshe Yeshiva in Chicago. Initially, he lived with the Levins, my brother- and sister-in-law and their sons. Our oldest daughter, Miriam, was also in Chicago, attending the girls' high school and living with my other brother and sister-in-law, the Kellers. Although these arrangements were satisfactory, Jackie and I were determined not to send our two younger daughters away from home for their adolescent years. So I began seriously considering positions in the New York area. I was very reluctant to leave Miami Beach, but I realized it was necessary. I received three job offers, none of which involved being a pulpit rabbi, which was a grave disappointment.

The first offer was to become the assistant to Rabbi Moshe Sherer, executive head of Agudath Israel of America. Rabbi Sherer was a family friend and especially close to Rabbi Leizer Levin, my father-in-law. In my opinion, Rabbi Sherer was the most outstanding Orthodox professional leader and administrator in American Jewry. Almost single-handedly, he built Agudath Israel into a major force in Orthodox life. He was a great man, but I was wary of becoming an assistant. The problem with assistants is that if they seem too capable, their superiors are threatened.

Rabbi Sherer told me that when he retired in a few years, I would succeed him. I politely declined the offer, though he and I remained friends and consulted each other for decades, until his death. (He never did retire, by the way.) Rabbi Sherer's greatness lay in his extraordinary administrative and communication skills, his vision and optimism regarding Orthodoxy in America, his shrewd political antennae, and, above all, his sterling character.

The second offer was from Rabbi Dr. Shmuel Belkin, head of Yeshiva University in New York. Rabbi Dr. Belkin was a friend of my father's from their time together in 1930 at RIETS, so he was somewhat prejudiced in my favor. The dean of students at RIETS, Rabbi Reuven Aberman, a friend from my Chicago yeshiva days, was moving to Israel in 1972 (where he later became a leading Torah educator). Rabbi Aberman recommended to Rabbi Dr. Belkin that I become the next dean of students. I met with Rabbi Dr. Belkin at his apartment on Central Park West in New York one day, but during the conversation I realized the job wasn't for me. I wouldn't be teaching, and administration alone didn't appeal to me. Yeshiva University was in financial trouble at the time, and I was afraid of that as well. To induce me to accept the offer, Rabbi Dr. Belkin promised he would assign someone to move my car whenever the street outside the yeshiva was cleaned. Not being a New Yorker, I didn't appreciate that perk. In any event, I politely declined the position.

I was immensely flattered that both Rabbi Sherer and Rabbi Dr. Belkin wanted me, even though in many respects their organizations were poles apart in outlook and policy.

The third offer was to become the executive vice president of the Orthodox Union. Rabbi Samson Raphael Weiss had served for many years in that position and was retiring to Israel. He had previously recommended me to the Queens synagogue mentioned earlier, and now he recommended me to the OU. I was warned that the position was really hollow and that I would be terribly frustrated. However, I rather naively thought I could greatly influence American Jewry, and I had big plans to build and strengthen Orthodox Judaism. I was officially appointed by the governing board and officers, and was to assume my duties on August 1, 1972.

My wife and I journeyed to New York repeatedly to find a house and community, without success. New York was too large and overwhelming for a family of hicks from Miami Beach. We liked a house in Far Rockaway, but "experts" told us the Jewish neighborhood was doomed. Today, against all odds and logic, it's thriving (and very expensive).

Jackie was partial to Monsey since she had a sister there, and its rural quality of life appealed to her much more than the bustle of New York City. A wealthy man in Miami Beach had told me he was selling his big house in Monsey, but the price was well beyond my means. Tragically, he died soon after our conversation, and his estate was tied up with many difficulties, leaving his widow quite cash-strapped. I assured her that I didn't want to take advantage of her situation, but my funds were limited. Incredibly, she agreed to my price. She was also kind enough to include an expensive dining room set and other furniture. (That dining room set is still in the home of one of my children almost forty years later.)

Now that we had a house and I had a good job in New York, we were ready to depart Miami Beach. Our years there were wonderful spiritually and physically. We were blessed to be there at a special time, serving very special people.

As mentioned, I had voluntarily taught Talmud to the eleventh grade of the Miami Mesivta. I loved teaching these bright young men, many of whom later became distinguished teachers, scholars, and rabbis. Some came from non-observant families and spent Shabbat and holidays in my home. I have met many of them later in life, and I remain inspired by their spiritual development, wonderful families, and meaningful contributions to the Jewish world.

Once, after discussing the complicated subject of halachic pedigrees that can disqualify someone from certain marriages, a young man in the class came to me and very tremulously said, "I'm afraid I have this pedigree problem." I flew to New York and discussed the issue with Rabbi Moshe Feinstein. He told me he would consider the matter when the boy was of marriageable age. The young man went on to study in excellent yeshivot and became a true scholar. About nine years later, I received a call from him that he was getting engaged and needed a letter from Rabbi Feinstein testifying to his acceptable pedigree. By then, as head of the ou Kashrut Division, I had consulted Rabbi Feinstein on countless issues without ever referring to this matter. Now, however, as I entered his study, he looked up at me and said sweetly, "You are here regarding the pedigree of that young man from Miami Beach. I have decided there is no problem." Cold Lithuanian though I am, I was shocked by this apparently supernatural event. A holy Jew is a holy Jew.

My mother passed away in Chicago on my last *erev Pesach* in Miami Beach (1972). She had suffered several minor strokes over the previous two years, leaving her with minor aphasia. Two days before Pesach, my father called to say she was back in the hospital. I flew to Chicago. My mother looked well and ready for discharge. My father had made arrangements to stay near the hospital for Pesach in case she wouldn't be released before the onset of the holiday. That night, I did *bedikat chametz* with my father in my parents' apartment and prepared to fly back to Miami Beach the next morning. At about midnight we received a call from the hospital that my mother had passed away. I somehow, almost miraculously, arranged for a funeral *erev Pesach* morning – and an early afternoon flight to Miami. My father and I arrived in Miami Beach a few hours before sunset.

Needless to say, it was quite a harrowing day. I still had *matzo shmura* packages I'd promised to deliver in Miami Beach, and I had to prepare myself and the house for the *Seder* and the holiday. Somehow everything was accomplished. My father conducted the *Seder* that night as though nothing had happened, though I know his heart was broken. Mother was only seventy years old.

I embarked upon the requisite year of mourning after the death of a parent. I had often wondered why children were to mourn a parent for a year, while for the surviving spouse a thirty-day mourning period was sufficient. I had my answer now. For the spouse, the pain and loss never disappear. However, children go on with their lives, and the loss of the parent fades more easily and quickly from daily life and consciousness. The mourning prescribed by *halachah* reflects these realities. The year of mourning allows a person to contemplate human mortality, as well as the role of parents and family in one's life; the resultant yearning for remembrance and immortality shapes our thoughts and deeds.

Our trip north to our new home in Monsey revolved around where a *minyan* could be found so I could recite *Kaddish*. Because of this issue, I had the strange feeling that my mother was somehow accompanying us on our new adventure. I felt comforted and strengthened by this thought.

Chapter 8

The New York Experience

"I learned a great deal about the practical application of halachah and about human character and motives."

Our new house was extraordinarily spacious, and our two younger daughters adjusted nicely to their new schools and made friends easily. Jackie became a fourth-grade teacher at the Yeshiva of Spring Valley, the large local day school that our daughters attended. She initially taught fourth-grade boys, but that proved far too challenging for her most gentle nature. So for the next twenty-four years, she taught fourth-grade girls with great skill and success.

I was very poorly prepared for the realities of our move to Monsey and for my new position as the executive vice president of the Orthodox Union. The salary I'd negotiated turned out to be far too low for the cost of living and commuting in the New York area. I tried to renegotiate, though it was abhorrent to my nature (as well as to the board of the OU), and did obtain some minimal relief. Nevertheless, we rapidly consumed all our savings and had to live much more simply than in Miami Beach. But my wife was very good at conserving our funds, and slowly we began saving money again for our eventual retirement.

My main difficulty was with the job itself. The Orthodox Union was located in a dingy building at 84 Fifth Avenue; the unkempt offices, poor lighting, and spartan furnishings were depressing.

The OU had five main divisions:

1. A division that dealt with public affairs, government bodies, and other Jewish and non-Jewish organizations
2. A synagogue division, which handled the needs and programs of the OU's member synagogues and organized national and regional conventions
3. A publications division, responsible chiefly for the production of *Jewish Life* magazine
4. The National Conference of Synagogue Youth (NCSY), a pioneering *kiruv* organization that operated a very successful network of youth programs, especially for public school students
5. A kashrut division

In theory, I was to coordinate and administer these divisions so they would form a harmonious whole. In practice, this proved impossible, since each operated as an independent fiefdom supported by different personalities and forces within the OU.

Another problem with my position was that I loathed the daily commute between Monsey and New York City. It took a minimum of an hour and fifteen minutes each way, and the traffic delays were nerve-wracking. My brother-in-law Rabbi Yaakov Lipschutz assisted Rabbi Alexander Rosenberg in the Kashrut Division, and together with two other Monsey residents who worked in Manhattan, we established a car pool. But the commute always took a heavy toll on my spirits and demeanor. I arrived at the office in the morning in a funk, and I came home to my family at night grumpy and exhausted. After a while, I forced myself to remain in my car for a few minutes before entering my home, to allow some of the negativity to drain out of me.

Winters in Monsey were pretty severe, with snow and ice underfoot for months on end. On many a frigid day I rued my decision to leave Miami Beach. But my children were happy, very popular, and receiving a good education, and my wife was also satisfied with our house and her teaching position, so I decided not to complain too much about my discomforts. New York City in the 1970s was in decline – dirty, dangerous, and depressing. I was not a happy camper.

After two months on the job, I realized that those who'd warned me about its downsides were correct. I was running from one fruitless meeting of pompous and mostly useless Jewish organizations to another. These groups were controlled by secular and Reform Jews who were openly antagonistic to the Orthodox community. I was accomplishing nothing on behalf of Torah and the Jewish People. Instead, I was reduced to writing speeches for others to deliver and attempting to manage an understaffed and financially strapped organization.

Ninety percent of the OU's income came from the Kashrut Division (which was much smaller than it is today), and there was little other fundraising. Almost none of the member synagogues paid their dues. The OU also paid for much of the upkeep of the Rabbinical Council of America. Everyone wanted a substantial piece of a relatively small pie. I could only juggle the conflicting obligations, never paying anyone on time.

I had signed a five-year contract with the OU, and I was grimly determined to honor it, though I gave notice early on that I didn't intend to serve any longer.

My only major project for the OU was the planning and organization of a national convention in November 1972. There was an unwritten understanding that Agudath Israel and the Orthodox Union would hold their conventions on alternate years to avoid competition. The OU's convention took place at the Boca Raton Hotel and Country Club (a venue once off-limits to Jews!) and was a great success both financially and socially. It was the hotel's first large Jewish and kosher affair. But this convention was my last hurrah as executive vice president of the Orthodox Union.

Rabbi Rosenberg, the rabbinic administrator of the OU Kashrut Division, died suddenly in Switzerland that autumn. Fierce competition and political maneuvering ensued as a successor was sought. To avoid chaos and protracted controversy, the chairman of the OU Kashrut Commission, Nathan K. Gross, asked me to replace him. Gross was a master politician (in the best sense of the word) and steered my unlikely candidacy through the maze of the OU's officers and board, obtaining the begrudging acceptance of the Rabbinical Council of America as well. I happily moved to the Kashrut Division, reiterating that I wouldn't serve beyond my five-year contract.

In 1972, the Kashrut Division had a very small office staff: two rabbinic coordinators and an excellent secretary. The number of companies and products under OU supervision was considerable – Rabbi Rosenberg had painstakingly built up this network over decades of service – albeit far smaller than the roster today. Financially, the division depended on four or five very large corporations that were always interested in expanding their kosher product line. They paid the OU out of their advertising budgets, not their manufacturing budgets, reasoning that instead of placing extravagant ads in Jewish publications, the OU symbol on their products would do the advertising for them. Anti-Jewish groups complained about the "Jewish tax" foisted upon them when they bought an OU-endorsed product. But this charge was patently false, since the advertising budget was fixed, and the monies paid to the OU were always in lieu of ads. I admired the companies that withstood these constant complaints and boycott threats. Many manufacturers even wrote back to these bigots, explaining their policy and why the "Jewish tax" was a malicious myth.

It was Rabbi Rosenberg's persona and integrity that granted the OU such a firm and cordial relationship with these corporations. His influence was astounding and continued long after his demise. A remarkable story comes to mind. In late 1973, after the Yom Kippur War, the Arab states launched an oil embargo of the West, especially the United States. Oil was crucial for the manufacture of kosher glycerin, a basic ingredient of many products under OU supervision. One day, I received a call from the plant manager of a large pharmaceutical company producing children's vitamins under OU supervision. The vitamins were part of a suspension liquid composed of 75 percent kosher glycerin. The manager informed me that the plant's supplier of kosher glycerin had run out of oil. He therefore had to switch to non-kosher glycerin. He also informed me that he had 100,000 labels bearing the OU symbol, and it would take two days to get new labels without it. He couldn't shut down his assembly line for two days. I asked how many tank cars of kosher glycerin he needed to use up the 100,000 labels, then told him I would call him back shortly.

I called the only other glycerin supplier in the United States under OU supervision and asked him – as a supreme favor – to ship the requisite quantity of kosher glycerin to the pharmaceutical company. The pharmaceutical company wasn't a regular customer of his, and I couldn't assure him that it ever would be. But I entreated him to help us out. He asked me, "Will Rabbi Rosenberg in Heaven know what I'm doing for you?" This non-Jewish officer of a major American corporation had no doubt that Rabbi Rosenberg was in Heaven and could pull strings for him! I responded that Heaven rewarded all good deeds and that his assistance would certainly be seen by Heaven and Rabbi Rosenberg as a good deed. The kosher glycerin was duly shipped, and the label crisis was averted. Even after the rabbi passed away, his clout upheld *kashrut* standards!

The Yom Kippur War itself was a tense and dangerous time for Jews the world over. My oldest daughter was then studying in Israel, having completed high school, and she experienced some worrisome events. We were all shocked by Israel's initial defeats and terribly frightened about the future of the Jewish State. President Richard M. Nixon and Secretary of State Henry Kissinger were hardly reassuring, and it was with great relief that we learned of the enemies' military reversal and the eventual Israeli victory.

Yet that victory launched the forty-year Arab drive to delegitimize Israel – which continues to this day – and the effort gained traction and momentum shortly after the war. An armed Yasser Arafat appeared on the podium of the United Nations, flaunting his pistol, and numerous nations began siding with the "Palestinians."

Around that time, the Military Rabbinate in Israel asked if I would represent it in certifying a few million cans of sardines ordered from Norway to replenish army rations consumed in the war. Norway wasn't allowing Israeli rabbis in to supervise production. So I flew to Stavanger, Norway. Stavanger in the winter is a cold, damp, dark, fishy-smelling, lonely place, but the experience was quite enlightening as far as food production is concerned. Every sardine was handled individually and checked for size and quality, and the tins were packed by hand! I arranged for the Orthodox rabbi of Copenhagen to supervise the plant, which now came under full OU supervision year-round, including Pesach.

At that point, importers in the United States wanted to bring in exotic French cheeses and wines, and they demanded OU supervision. So I visited France and met with the Paris *beit din* as well as with the competing *Charedi* body. Great tact and delicacy were always required in making arrangements between competing rabbinic organizations for a common OU supervision process. Most of life is turf. The fact that I was known to be apolitical – and *Charedi* yet modern – confused many rabbis but always stood me in good stead. The older rabbis in France were initially somewhat suspicious of me – they felt I was too young and American to be relied on in *kashrut* decisions – but eventually I allayed their fears. Proper rabbinic supervision was instituted, and the spiritual and monetary issues were settled to the satisfaction of all concerned.

There was, and is, big money involved in *kashrut* supervision. Since the OU was a public organization and everyone involved in *kashrut* supervision received a fixed salary, irrespective of new or old business considerations, the system was virtually incorruptible. Rabbi Rosenberg's personal integrity permeated the organization. He had refused all gifts and favors from OU-certified companies and I continued that policy.

I remember an incident that became a defining moment for me in my public and private life. An Orthodox Jewish man was opening a food establishment in New York in two weeks and requested OU certification. Rabbi Rosenberg told him that the process of obtaining OU certification could not be completed within two weeks. The man persisted and blatantly offered him 5 percent of the stock in the new corporation if he would expedite the process. Rabbi Rosenberg remained silent, looking heavenward. The man took the rabbi's silence as a negotiating tactic and raised his offer to 7 percent. Rabbi Rosenberg then looked at him and said in Yiddish, *"Un voss zogt Gott dertzu?* – And what do you think God would say about our conversation?"

The rabbi later remarked to me, "Would he have spoken that way if he'd thought the Internal Revenue Service was listening in?"

Rabbi Rosenberg was a pillar of integrity, and he built the OU on his principles. He was always aware that money is the great corrupter in all religious life and society. His chief concern about rabbis offering private kosher supervision was that they were operating for personal profit and, as such, always susceptible to corruption. Nevertheless, he helped many competing *kashrut* certifiers, even those who constantly belittled the OU's standards while using OU-certified plants and products for goods under their supposedly superior supervision. In almost all instances, I continued his policies. I learned very early on that, unfortunately, there was a great deal of hypocrisy and outright extortion and false claims in the field of *kashrut* supervision. The OU, under both Rabbi Rosenberg and me, refused to certify companies that merely repackaged OU products under their own label, then raised the price with the claim that their brand was "more kosher" than the competing OU item. I resented these holy hypocrites; but they could always find a rabbi or *rebbe* who would put his name on their package. They relied on OU *kashrut* even as they badmouthed the OU! But I learned to live with the situation and not become too exercised over it.

For years, much-needed kosher products had essentially been subsidized by the OU. No company could afford to maintain the organization's *kashrut* standards, so many of the supervisors, rabbis, and inspectors assigned to plants were paid by the OU itself. People often criticized the OU for certifying detergents and other patently non-food items that apparently required no *kashrut* supervision;[1] yet these certifications enabled the OU to supervise such staples as matzo and poultry, though still at considerable expense and monetary loss.

The main kosher poultry provider in the United States was Empire, operated by a father and son, Joe and Murray Katz. The Katzes were not especially observant Jews, but they never questioned our *kashrut* standards, and enforced all the rulings of the OU rabbinic staff unwaveringly. I regularly visited their two main plants, in Mifflintown and the aptly named Bird-in-Hand, both located in the Amish country of Pennsylvania. I established very good relations with the Katzes and their *shochtim*. (Their Amish neighbors dressed just like the *shochtim*, in wide-brimmed, black hats and long, black frocks and beards. But the *shochtim* had mustaches, while the Amish men didn't.) I became proficient at inspecting the *shechitah* knives and supervising all the procedures necessary to uphold the OU's high *kashrut* standards. The plants

---

1. The manufacturers knew these products required no certification. Nevertheless, they wanted brand identification with the kosher consumer and a uniform labeling policy. Therefore, *they* demanded supervision. The OU symbol improved their shelf position in supermarkets serving a large Jewish population, which resulted in far greater sales than could be attributed to the Jewish market itself.

also produced poultry for other *kashrut*-certifying organizations, and I negotiated and smoothed out relations with them as well. No *kashrut* standards were more stringent than the OU's.

When Joe Katz passed away, my wife and I were on a long-planned vacation. The Katz family somehow reached me at our motel and asked me to officiate at the funeral. I quickly returned to New York to accommodate this request. Thanks to Joe Katz, the Katz family was committed to the production and distribution of kosher poultry in America, not only as a business but as a worthwhile cause in itself. Katz deserved the respect and honor of the OU at his funeral. This wasn't the first or last time I cut short a vacation to attend to rabbinic duties.

During my years as rabbinic administrator, I flew a lot. Interesting things always seem to occur on my travels, providing me with lots of airplane stories. In early 1974, when the Arab oil embargo of America was in full force, I was seated on a plane next to a very well-dressed businesswoman. In mid-flight, without warning, she turned to me and said, "You know, all this trouble we're in is your fault." America was suffering from a major gasoline shortage, with long lines at every gas station, bringing much latent anti-Semitism to the fore. Yet I was taken aback by the nature and tone of her words. Somehow, I very calmly answered her, "No, madam. It may be because of me, but it is definitely not my fault." We said nothing more for the rest of the flight.

Remember: Much may happen in human society and history for which the Jewish People may be the catalyst, but in no way does that make us at fault for what occurs. This crucial subtlety underpins all intelligent appraisals of Jewish history.

I was once scheduled to fly to Atlanta to speak at a fundraising banquet for the local day school. I had booked a flight with the now defunct but then newly bankrupt TWA. I arrived at the airport with what I thought was plenty of time, but because of the bankruptcy, TWA had only one ticket agent to handle the many dozens of customers in line. After standing in line more than an hour, I finally arrived at the counter, only to be informed that the computer automatically erased reservations a half hour before flight time – and it was now twenty-eight minutes before flight time. I implored the agent to overlook the two minutes, and she finally relented. She assigned me the last available seat on the plane – 3A in first class. I ran to the gate and boarded the plane just as the door was closing. When the flight attendant saw my seat assignment, she whispered to me, "You're sitting next to the vice president of the airline."

Sure enough, when I arrived breathlessly at row 3, the vice president had strewn spreadsheets over both seats and was busy futilely attempting to save the airline. I asked to sit in seat 3A. He very reluctantly gathered up his papers and gave me a dour look as I plopped into my seat. After the plane took off, he again took out all his paperwork and went to work. I, in turn, took out my *Chumash* to look over the week's *parshah*. After a few moments, he leaned over and asked, "What language is that book written in?"

"Hebrew," I answered sweetly.

"You mean there are still people left in the world who read and write Hebrew?" he responded incredulously. "I thought it was a dead language."

"Well," I explained, "there are millions of people in the world who read, write, and speak Hebrew. In fact, your airline flies regularly to a country where Hebrew is the official language for millions of people."

For some reason he disliked my response. "I see that you and I have nothing in common," he muttered, turning away.

"That's not true," I countered. "We have an important matter in common."

"What's that?" he snarled.

"Neither of us paid for this first-class seat."

The rest of the flight passed in silence between us.

After the Israeli raid on Entebbe, in the summer of 1976, my rabbinic coordinator, Rabbi Lipschutz, and I were scheduled to fly to Japan, then Tehran, and then on to Israel on OU business. Our trip to Japan was relatively uneventful but fascinating. Because of the halachic dispute regarding the location of the International Date Line, it's unclear whether Shabbat in Japan is on Saturday or Sunday. We therefore spent a fifty-hour "Shabbat" in Nara, Japan: On Sunday, we put on *tefillin* but continued refraining from all labor prohibited on Shabbat.[2]

---

2. Nara is a holy city for many Japanese, in which their ancestors' spirits supposedly

We also stayed in a 950-year-old inn near Kyoto where there were no locks on the door, futon mats were our beds, and an elaborate tea ceremony was performed in our room every afternoon. Negotiating a contract with the Japanese was also an experience: They have infinite patience and generally remain silent. Thus the American (always eager to close the deal) usually ends up negotiating with himself, to his own financial detriment. In our case, a Japanese glycerin manufacturer wanted kosher certification. The company intended to export to Israel, but wouldn't allow any Israeli rabbis to come certify the product. So the OU stepped in, as it often did in such sensitive diplomatic situations.

As mentioned, we were to fly from Japan to Tehran. The tickets on Pan Am were Tokyo-Bangkok-New Delhi-Tehran. Then I saw an ad in the English-language newspaper in Tokyo that Air Iran had just begun direct flights from Tokyo to Tehran, saving nine hours. We switched our tickets, without knowing this "direct" flight would stop in Beijing. Nixon and Kissinger had just opened up China, yet Americans still dared not visit.

When we landed in Beijing, a Chinese army captain and soldier, weapons drawn, boarded the plane and swiftly collected all passports. Since we had no entry visas to China, we were summarily hauled off the plane and marched to the terminal. The building was dimly lit and bare, except for an enormous portrait of Chairman Mao gazing at us benevolently. I was frightened, because no one knew we were in Beijing; everyone in America had only our original Pan Am itinerary.

In perfect English, the captain directed us to a bench while he inquired what to do. A series of frantic phone calls in Chinese ensued between him and his superiors. We were asked if we knew any language besides English. We said no. And what were we doing in China, since we'd come from the US and were en route to Israel, neither of which had diplomatic relations with this country? I explained that we didn't know Air Iran stopped in Beijing, and that we had no intention of staying in China. The captain's secretary then told me in Spanish (I knew some from my Miami Beach days) that if we each gave her ten American dollars, she

---

inhabit the bodies of the midget deer that roam freely (even in the hotel lobby). The deer expect to be fed, even nosing around in people's pockets for food!

would arrange visas for us. Since I had said I knew only English, I didn't respond. More phone calls. Finally the captain himself stated that for ten dollars each we could obtain visas allowing us to enter China for six hours.

We gladly paid the money and were then marched back to the plane, which thankfully, after ninety minutes, was still waiting for us. We were instructed to walk straight to the aircraft and not look back or even around us. When we finally were back onboard, the relief of the crew and passengers was palpable. A few moments later, the captain returned our passports, now containing newly issued visas. The relief and thankfulness I felt when the plane finally took off remain among the deepest emotions I have ever felt.

As mentioned, New York in the mid-1970s was unsafe. Our office building was poorly guarded; anyone could gain access. One evening, at about 6:30 pm, a number of us were still working in the office (attempting to catch up, as we often did, on the voluminous and tedious paperwork necessitated by the OU's *kashrut* operations). A tall, black man brandishing a knife entered our office and took everything of value, including a very expensive watch given to me by my Miami Beach congregation. Then he cut the phone wires and warned us not to leave the office for another half hour and to forget about contacting the police. After we finally did leave, shaken and somewhat dazed, we reported the robbery. As usual at the time, the police seemed uninterested, and we never heard from them. Two weeks later, I spotted the robber on the street in front of our building – he apparently liked our neighborhood – and immediately reported his presence and a detailed description to the police. Again nothing happened. After this, I didn't allow our staff to stay alone late in the building or to come in on Sunday, however pressing the workload. I also resolved never to wear expensive watches again.

Nevertheless, the lay Kashrut Commission continued holding its monthly meetings at night in our offices, despite my recommendation to move them to safer quarters. This body evidently felt it had Divine protection – though its rabbinic staff did not.

I abhor controversy and have always gone out of my way to avoid it. As rabbinic administrator, however, I had to meet monthly with the

Kashrut Committee of the Rabbinical Council of America, an organization founded in the 1930s as an alternate to the Orthodox Union, which was then dominated by Eastern European rabbis. The RCA consisted overwhelmingly of graduates of Yeshiva University. Having never attended that institution, I was treated as an outsider, if not an interloper. I always sensed hostility toward me, real or imagined. Several rabbis on the committee were openly, constantly critical of me as well as my decisions and proposals. I attributed this undeserved animosity to personal pique stemming from Rabbi Rosenberg's battles with the committee. Moreover, my position was erroneously assumed to be well-paid, with many perks attached.

The executive vice president of the RCA was Rabbi Israel Klavan, a very shrewd and astute leader, and a close confidant of Rabbi Joseph B. Soloveitchik, the spiritual head of YU. To minimize the constant friction between the OU and the RCA, Rabbi Klavan advised me to cultivate a personal relationship with Rabbi Soloveitchik.

I was not a student of Rabbi Soloveitchik's, but I had attended classes and lectures he'd delivered in Miami Beach, and he knew of me. I began visiting him regularly in his apartment in YU's Morgenstern Residence Hall. I attended his famous *yahrzeit* lectures and spent a week every summer at his vacation home near Cape Cod, listening to his teachings. I called him regularly, sharing personal and OU issues with him. He was unfailingly kind and generous to me, always giving me time and advice. His private persona was much different from his public one, and I always felt relaxed and open speaking with him. He protected my flank from the critics of the OU, both internally as well as in the RCA. By the end of my five-year stint as rabbinic administrator, my critics and I were reconciled, and many even became friends and cooperative colleagues. I attribute that achievement to my relationship with Rabbi Soloveitchik and his constant support of me, which became widely known in rabbinic circles.

When I became the rabbinic administrator, I discovered that the OU supervised the commissary preparing the kosher meals for El Al Airlines. The company was delivering food to the airline on Shabbat so planes could make a quick departure on Saturday night. (This was before El Al stopped flying on Shabbat, and its attitude toward traditional observance was very tepid.) The OU-appointed rabbi who supervised the *kashrut* at that commissary was a well-known scholar, yet – apparently unbeknownst to Rabbi Rosenberg – he allowed these Shabbat deliveries. I met with him a few times, and he finally agreed not to allow any deliveries until at least forty-five minutes after sunset on Saturday night. Consequently, El Al had to postpone its Saturday night flight by two hours.

Well, all hell broke loose. I was accused of being anti-Zionist. Israeli government ministers called me and protested vehemently. Religious politicians and members of Knesset pressured the RCA to have the ruling changed or have me fired. All because of a relatively slight change in the flight schedule! It was the principle of the thing, they claimed: No rabbi was going to tell Israel's national airline what to do. No "religious coercion."

At the next RCA Kashrut Committee meeting, I recommended that the matter be referred to Rabbi Soloveitchik. A few days later, the Rav informed me that he had received a phone call from Israel's minister of transportation about the later deliveries. "Rabbi Wein," he said, "do you know what I told him?" I eagerly awaited his next statement. "I said, 'If you were Swissair, perhaps I could find a leniency on your behalf. But for El Al there is no such leniency!'" And that ended the matter permanently.

As the rabbi of Boston, Rabbi Soloveitchik certified the *kashrut* of many food products produced there, including meat. Under Rabbi Rosenberg's policies, some of these products didn't meet OU standards and therefore couldn't be used in OU-certified establishments. In the RCA Kashrut Committee meetings, I was constantly criticized for not changing Rabbi Rosenberg's policies regarding these products. Some accused me of outright disrespect for Rabbi Soloveitchik in not accepting all products bearing his name. In all my meetings with the Rav, I never discussed this sensitive matter with him. However, he once said to me, "As the rabbi of Boston, it is my duty to grant *kashrut* certification to products that are kosher, even if they don't necessarily reach the highest standards of *kashrut*. I know you have to operate under a different set of rules. Don't be troubled that the OU doesn't use certain products I certify. I'm not troubled by it." I never revealed that conversation to the Kashrut Committee, nor did I change OU policy.

Rabbi Soloveitchik once told me that all the rabbis he knew were basically fine, sincere people. Yet he wondered aloud why, when they met as a group or committee, their behavior was often unacceptable and impractical. I recalled an anecdote that Rabbi Aaron Paperman once related to me. He and Rabbi Mordechai Gifter (later the *rosh yeshiva* of Telshe Yeshiva in Cleveland) were students at the yeshiva in Telshe, Lithuania, in the late 1930s. As war clouds gathered, their families in America insisted that they return to the United States. Yet Rabbis Paperman and Gifter wanted to attend an upcoming rabbinic convention in Lithuania first. When they asked Rabbi Avraham Yitzchak Bloch, the rabbi and *rosh yeshiva* of Telshe, for permission to do so, he demurred. Being determined Americans, they pestered him again for permission to attend the convention. This time Rabbi Bloch answered them more sharply: "I don't understand you. What do you wish to see? Great people at their pettiest (*gedolim b'katnusam*)?"

Throughout my career, I have avoided rabbinic conventions, except when I've been a scheduled speaker or otherwise obligated to attend. I don't say this course is correct for anyone else. It is merely a personal peculiarity of which I am neither particularly proud nor ashamed.

Rabbi Moshe Feinstein truly carried the Jewish People in his heart and on his slight shoulders. As mentioned, I visited his modest apartment on Manhattan's Lower East Side fairly regularly. Guided by his wisdom and erudition, I was able to clarify a number of halachic issues regarding poultry and meat production (especially concerning temporary lesions commonly found in the intestines of Cornish hens). At my initiative, the OU began certifying beef production at kosher slaughterhouses. Many of the older European rabbis who privately supervised most of the meat plants throughout the country opposed the entry of the OU into the field. In conversations with me, Rabbi Feinstein supported their position. Therefore, only two slaughterhouses, in Philadelphia and in York, Nebraska, came under OU supervision during my tenure. In both cases, the older rabbis acquiesced to the OU's entry and retained a paid, supervisory role at those plants. I told Rabbi Feinstein that I had no intention of bringing more such plants under OU supervision and that the small-scale meat production we supervised (mainly for Satmar and other Hasidic groups) met our needs.

(Certifying such slaughterhouses was very challenging, however. Rabbi Shlomo Zweigenhaft was mainly responsible for implementing OU standards. He had studied under Rabbi Zvi Frommer, head of the famed yeshiva in Lublin after the death of its founder, Rabbi Meir Shapiro. Rabbi Zweigenhaft was an expert in all the halachic and practical issues of kosher meat production. He was also a wonderful human being and rapidly became a very good friend.)

During those years, Rabbi Feinstein had a personal secretary, Rabbi Moshe Rivlin, who protected him from uninvited visitors. Once a woman arrived and loudly demanded to see Rabbi Feinstein immediately. The woman wasn't dressed properly for a visit with a rabbi, and she wouldn't tell Rabbi Rivlin the purpose of her unscheduled visit. He refused her admission, but she created such a tumult that Rabbi Feinstein himself opened the door to his study to see what the problem was. He ushered the woman into his room, where she remained for about twenty minutes. As she left, she chastised his secretary for denying her immediate entry. Rabbi Rivlin apologized and asked what was so pressing. She replied, "I live upstairs, and whenever I receive a letter from my relatives in Israel, Rabbi Feinstein reads it for me and explains its contents." For great people there is no such thing as a small favor for another Jew – everything is important.

I always left Rabbi Feinstein's home uplifted and inspired. He was unfailingly gentle and friendly, patient, unhurried, and sympathetic, and he clearly recognized the importance of the OU in American Jewish life. Sometimes I felt frustrated by his favoring the older European rabbis over what I considered more practical and progressive directions in *kashrut*, but I always obeyed him. Rabbi Rosenberg had disagreed with him about OU standards regarding canned tuna, and I upheld the former's policy. But I never raised the issue with him, nor did he ever speak to me about it. Rabbi Feinstein was the quintessential scholar, humanitarian, and Jewish leader – cloaked within great humility and holiness. He was practicality and vision combined. I feel privileged to have known him.

On the whole, despite the torturous daily commute from Monsey and back, the frequent travel, and the tensions, politics, and latent controversies inherent in the position, I enjoyed my stint as the OU rabbinic administrator. I learned a great deal about the practical application of *halachah* and about human character and motives. And because of my legal experience, I had the opportunity to draw up standard contracts and forms to cover OU certification as well as the sale of *chametz* before Pesach.

As mentioned, by the end of my five-year contract with the Orthodox Union, I had reconciled with my adversaries, real or imagined – it's easy to become paranoid in such a position – and apologized to those I felt I had wronged. My colleagues showed me great kindness, and many – including Rabbis Soloveitchik and Klavan – urged me to reconsider my departure, as did Nathan K. Gross and Julius Berman of the lay Kashrut Commission. There was no real mechanism for finding someone to replace me. To a certain extent, no one actually believed I was leaving. Some even thought I was bluffing as a negotiating tactic.

But I was determined to reenter the more gratifying field of the pulpit rabbinate and Jewish education. I was convinced that the OU Kashrut Division would continue to expand and thrive and that a worthy successor would emerge. Those hopes have been amply fulfilled over the many decades since. American, Israeli, and world Jewry owe a vast and eternal debt of gratitude to the OU for making kosher food plentiful and available almost everywhere – all at the highest halachic standards. I am very proud and grateful to have been part of that illustrious story.

Chapter 9

Up and Down the Hill in Monsey

"I have always been inordinately proud of the generations of children raised in Bais Torah."

A hamlet next to the village of Spring Valley, New York, Monsey was a farming community where kosher hotels had taken root. Five degrees cooler in the summer than New York City, it was closer to the city than the Catskills. In time, beyond filling the hotels, many Jews bought or rented small homes – essentially bungalows – for summer use. Some of these hardy people, loving the rural openness of the place, winterized their homes and became year-round residents.

The population grew in the 1940s, when Rabbi Shraga Feivel Mendlowitz, head of Yeshiva Torah Vodaath, established a *kollel* for outstanding young scholars in Monsey: Beis Medrash Elyon, headed by Rabbi Reuven Grozovsky. Many of these students eventually settled in Monsey permanently.

Monsey benefited greatly from the Tappan Zee Bridge (connecting Rockland and Westchester counties since 1955) as well as the 1958 extension of the Palisades Parkway all the way up to Nanuet, granting direct access to the George Washington Bridge into New York City. With the daily commute made that much easier, most Monsey men worked in the city. The trip wasn't necessarily pleasant once the roads became crowded, but when I moved to Monsey it was still tolerable. Jewish bus companies began commuter runs as well, picking up passengers in Monsey and dropping them off in Manhattan and Brooklyn. Catering to commuters' early-hour needs, some buses even offered a daily *minyan* (necessitating a *mechitzah*), which became famous – and sometimes infamous – over the years. At any rate, with increased transportation options, the Jewish population of Monsey rose steadily, and by the 1970s, it had grown into a significant Jewish enclave.

There were three groups of Orthodox Jews in Monsey. Two of them – Hasidic and "yeshivish" (originally connected mainly to Beis Medrash Elyon) – lived primarily "down the hill" in lower Monsey. Then there were the more "modern" Orthodox Jews, many of them graduates of Yeshiva University, who lived "up the hill." The hill (traversed by Maple Avenue) was a formidable climb, both physically and socially.

The Yeshiva of Spring Valley, a large elementary school established in the 1940s, and Beis Shraga, a yeshiva high school established by Rabbi Mendlowitz's son, were located down the hill. Another elementary school geared primarily to the Hasidic population, Beis David, was down the hill as well. Up the hill, there was a Zionist, Hebrew-oriented day school, the Hebrew Institute of Rockland County (HIROC, later the Adolph Schreiber Hebrew Academy of Rockland, ASHAR), and a small yeshiva founded and headed by the Zaks family, descendants of the Chofetz Chaim's son-in-law.

There were a number of synagogues down the hill, including a spinoff of New York City's German Washington Heights community. Up the hill, there was the large Community Synagogue of Monsey, led by Rabbi Moshe Tendler, son-in-law of Rabbi Moshe Feinstein. There were also regular services in the HIROC building as well as in the Chofetz Chaim Yeshiva building. Neither of these prayer groups had an official rabbi. This was the Monsey to which my family and I moved in the summer of 1972.

Our house was "up the hill," and I attended the Community Synagogue of Monsey. Some of our neighbors, with whom we very quickly became good friends, *davened* at Yeshiva Chofetz Chaim, which was much closer to our home. They soon asked me to teach a Torah class on Shabbat afternoons. Since the *minyan* had no rabbi, I naively agreed.

The class proved too popular. After a few weeks, the head of the yeshiva objected to my teaching in his building without his permission. I had more than enough strife from my day job at the OU, so I discontinued the class and began attending Shabbat services in the HIROC building. Many of those who prayed and studied with me at the yeshiva *minyan* now showed up at the HIROC *minyan*. Once again, I was asked to conduct a Shabbat afternoon class and I foolishly agreed to do so, not having learned my lesson that rabbinic newcomers to Monsey were not especially welcome. Like the old adage about children – they were to be seen but not heard.

Again, the class proved very popular. Soon I was visited by a delegation of lay leaders of HIROC. They stated that there was "rabbinical objection" as well as resistance in the school community to my teaching. For the benefit of the community, would I perhaps consider moving out of Monsey?

I quickly took the hint and accepted a position as the Shabbat rabbi at the Young Israel of Riverdale, in the Bronx. I also sold my home and began looking for an apartment in Riverdale.

But my Monsey friends and neighbors begged me not to leave. They committed themselves to creating a synagogue in our area where I would be the rabbi. They understood that my job with the OU took precedence. They even saw to it that the buyer of my home backed out, and negotiated a graceful exit for me from my agreement with the Young Israel of Riverdale.

Bais Torah began with forty families, and I was paid very nominally. But it was a wonderful group, and I was enthusiastic about prospects for the synagogue's growth and influence in the community.

Of course, some members of the OU Kashrut Commission objected to my moonlighting. I responded that they were paying me rather meagerly, and that in all his years as rabbinic administrator, Rabbi Rosenberg was also the rabbi of a synagogue in Yonkers. They all agreed that I was doing a good job and, I argued, my being a practicing rabbi only enhanced the prestige of the OU's rabbinic administrator. Besides, nothing in my contract with the OU precluded my taking a rabbinic position while serving as rabbinic administrator. The issue never went away, but neither did it become a great bone of contention.

Over time, I noticed that being the rabbi of Bais Torah, teaching Torah regularly, and interacting with people who wanted to grow spiritually all helped me cope with the pressures of my administrative position with the OU. Bais Torah gave me fulfillment and happiness that translated into positive behavior and a more pleasant, less contentious atmosphere at the OU offices.

Things soon settled down in Monsey. The congregation began meeting in a large basement. The wags called our synagogue Bais Ment. Yet membership grew, and the *shul* purchased a rhubarb farm just outside Monsey, in Suffern. The farmhouse was refurbished by synagogue volunteers. The congregation rapidly outgrew those quarters too, and built an attractive, wooden structure that could hold the hundreds of worshipers that now attended Bais Torah. After several years, a further building expansion took place, and Bais Torah became one of the leading synagogues in the Monsey area. When I went to town hall with the building plans for our synagogue, the supervisor queried, "Do you think a non-Orthodox synagogue such as yours can succeed in your location?" I asked him why he thought the synagogue wasn't Orthodox. He answered me in all seriousness, "There's no request for a zoning variance or waiver attached to your application." Bais Torah always did things by the book.

Dedicating a *sefer Torah* to the synagogue (Suffern, NY, 1988)

Rabbi Yaakov Kamenetsky was one of Monsey's greatest assets. He was one of the great men of the generation, a Torah genius, and one of the wisest people I've ever met. I knew him from Miami Beach and visited him many times in his small house "down the hill," always attempting to judiciously follow his instructions and advice. Nevertheless, he continually emphasized that all the decisions in question were mine, and that no rabbinic figure had the right to impose his will upon others. He was a mainstay and a great support to me in all my endeavors. He attended the groundbreaking ceremony for the construction of the new *shul* edifice and spoke generously of me and my congregation.

To a certain extent, Rabbi Kamenetsky was the "last of the Mohicans" in the Lithuanian yeshiva world that I belonged to, which clearly limited rabbinic authority over others' actions, thoughts, and opinions. Because of this attitude, I respected his opinions, perhaps more than otherwise would have been the case. I'm no rebel or seeker of controversy. Nevertheless, I've always treasured my independence of thought and behavior (all within the confines of Jewish tradition and *halachah*, of course). Human beings are not robots, and the Talmud allows that "as their countenances differ, so do their opinions." Freedom of choice is a cornerstone of Judaism.

Because of my frequent visits to Rabbi Kamenetsky, I witnessed some memorable displays of his humor. He had great wit and practicality. A young man once asked how he would know which woman had been set aside for him to marry according to Heaven's proclamation forty days before his birth. With a twinkle in his eye and a smile on his lips, Rabbi Kamenetsky triumphantly said to him, "That's what they call love."

Another time, someone asked which of two surgeons he should engage for a pending operation. One was Jewish and the other wasn't. Rabbi Kamenetsky advised him to go to the best surgeon, irrespective of his religious or ethnic background. "What if they're equal?" the man pressed. Rabbi Kamenetsky replied that he doubted this was the case, but if the man felt so, he should probably prefer the Jewish surgeon. The man countered, "What if there are two Jewish surgeons, but one is an observant Jew and the other isn't?" The rabbi reiterated that he should go to the best surgeon. But the questioner persisted, "What if the two are equal?" Rabbi Kamenetsky once more doubted this would be the case, but said that if the man felt so strongly about it, he should go to the observant surgeon. The person then said to him, "How could I do that? He ignored the opinion of many *roshei yeshiva* and attended medical school!" The rabbi quickly replied, "It is one of God's beneficent miracles that not everyone listens to us."

I learned a great deal just being with Rabbi Kamenetsky. Though *nudniks* were constantly bothering him – I also probably fell into that category – he never lost his composure, good humor, and kindness toward others.

I once drove Rabbi Kamenetsky and his wife to a wedding in New York City. The wait at the George Washington Bridge was long and frustrating as usual. When I finally reached the toll booth, I gave the clerk a twenty-dollar bill. He gave me the proper change, and I zoomed out of the toll area and onto the bridge. Rabbi Kamenetsky gently leaned over and said quietly, "Rabbi Wein, you forgot to say thank you to the toll taker for the proper change he gave you." I have never since crossed over that bridge without hearing Rabbi Kamenetsky's words in my mind.

I resolved to work with all the rabbis of Monsey, both up and down the hill. I was fairly successful, especially after leaving the ou, for I shed the image of the "important" national administrator that sometimes alienated local rabbis. In addition, I no longer represented a competitor to any *kashrut*-certifying organization, each of which had Monsey connections and personnel. I assisted the Rebbe of New Square regarding a difficult legal matter. I also helped Vishnitz, a large, Hasidic community down the hill, with zoning and town affairs. I aided the Yeshiva of Spring Valley and HIROC as well. And I helped support all the other educational institutions up and down the hill, as well as many local charities.

I worked hard to build these bridges. Eventually, even those who were less than enthusiastic about my arrival in Monsey became my colleagues and friends. Together, we sold the community's *chametz*, built an *eruv* (no, it wasn't universally accepted – but what *eruv* is?), and maintained a *beit din* to adjudicate disputes.

This was no small task. Jewish history over the centuries is littered with rabbis driven from their communities by powerful, dissatisfied litigants. One such even sued me, accusing me of bias and even indirectly of graft. Ultimately, the civil court agreed with the *beit din*, but I suffered great aggravation over the matter. No wonder many rabbis refuse to sit on a *beit din*. Unlike the hagiographic biographies of great rabbinic personalities, no rabbi I know ever encountered a wrathful litigant and escaped unscathed. Such is life, certainly in communities like Monsey.

Though I received many offers after leaving the OU – some of them lucrative – to grant kosher supervision to certain companies and establishments, I abstained from all *kashrut* supervision. I've always felt strongly that only national or local non-profit rabbinic organizations should be in the *kashrut* field, not private entrepreneurs. The periodic *kashrut* scandals in Monsey and elsewhere concerning establishments and individuals under private supervision have only confirmed my opinion. But that's only my personal policy. I have nothing against those who provide *hechsherim* (*kashrut* certifications).

On Sunday mornings, Bais Torah permitted a representative of needy institutions or individuals to say a few words from the pulpit and appeal for money. I was cautioned that this practice would reduce attendance at our Sunday morning *minyan*, but it didn't. Bais Torah gained a well-deserved reputation as a bastion of charity as well as an outstanding house of prayer and study.

I put special effort into my hour-long Shabbat Hagadol and Shabbat Shuva lectures at Bais Torah. The *shul* was always filled during these sermons, attracting many people from all over Monsey who were not members of our synagogue. I spoke in the classical style I'd learned from my father – meshing serious halachic issues and "lighter" aggadic interpretations. I often worked a whole month on each lecture, until it was good and presentable.

The High Holiday services at Bais Torah were special – almost electric. In the month prior to the holidays, I would teach the genius of the prayers to my congregants. The synagogue always had excellent, inspiring, and vocally gifted leaders of the melodious services; the *shofar* blowing was extraordinary; the atmosphere was serious and emotional.

The singing in unison of the traditional melodies and the excellent voices and intonations of the prayer leaders combined to make the *davening* dramatic and soaring, filled with concentration and holy intent. Many guests and relatives of members of Bais Torah attended these High Holiday services, and they often commented on their special experience in that wooden structure on the outskirts of Monsey. Many years later, children raised in Bais Torah told me that the High Holidays in our *shul* made an enormous, lasting impression on them.

I have always been inordinately proud of the generations of children raised in Bais Torah. On Shabbat afternoons I taught Mishnah to groups of boys. The younger group comprised six- to nine-year-olds, and the older group was for ages nine to twelve. I had about twenty boys in each group, and at the end of the half-hour class I distributed sour balls. Some boys asked for candies for their siblings at home, and I always accommodated them – even when I knew there were no siblings at home. Some "cheated" by staying for both classes to get candy twice. I always pretended not to notice. Candy once got stuck in a boy's trachea, and he started to choke. I administered the Heimlich maneuver, and he revived nicely – but I resolved to give out softer sweets thereafter. I conducted these Shabbat classes for twenty-four years, and generations of young men passed through our home.

My wife ran Shabbat groups for the girls of the synagogue and produced an annual play with them, much as she had in Miami Beach, which was always a great favorite. The show proved so popular and well known in Monsey that several families actually joined our *shul* so their daughters could participate in Jackie's productions.

As in Miami Beach, we had wonderful neighbors in Monsey. In Miami Beach, a delightful older woman, Mrs. Geller, delivered a freshly baked challah to us every Friday afternoon. My wife happened to mention this in passing to two of our neighbors, the Hammers and the Levins, and for the next (nearly) forty years, they arranged that a freshly baked challah be delivered on Friday afternoon to our home in Monsey, and then in Jerusalem.

As the children grew up and the two eldest were studying away from home, our enormous house was too big for us. It cost a fortune to heat it in the winter and cool it in the summer, and it was hard and expensive to clean and maintain it. The front and back lawns were huge and required constant attention and maintenance.

Our older daughter, Miriam, became engaged to Yisrael Gettinger, the oldest son of Rabbi and Mrs. Emmanuel Gettinger. Rabbi Gettinger was the longtime rabbi of the Young Israel of the West Side in New York City. Since this was a wedding of the children of two community rabbis, many guests were invited, and about 750 people actually attended. To help pay for the wedding, my wife and I put our large house up for sale; it sold quickly and at a good price. With the profits, we paid our share of the wedding expenses, while the principal was reinvested in a smaller home in the neighborhood.

We found a house at the top of the "hill" in Monsey, only a ten-minute walk from the synagogue. However, the previous owner had suffered family tragedies there, and the buzz in Monsey was that the home was somehow cursed. No one would buy it. But we really liked the place, and my Lithuanian upbringing led me to scorn stories of demons and cursed houses. I offered a price I could afford, and the seller readily accepted. He was thrilled to have found a Litvak to take it off his hands!

When it became known in Monsey – and in Monsey everything becomes known fast – that I had contracted to buy the house, the phone calls poured in. The common message was that it was a cursed house and I shouldn't buy it. Many callers were people I had never met. I was immensely flattered that so many cared about my welfare. To dispel any doubts, Jackie and I consulted Rabbi Kamenetsky. He asked my wife, "Do you like the house?" She answered that yes, she liked it very much. He then asked me, "Is it a fair price?" When I answered in the affirmative, he looked at us with a big smile and said, "So what's the problem?"

We bought the house. The day after we moved in, others offered to buy it at a sizable profit. People apparently figured that somehow – perhaps through my actually purchasing and living in the place even for one day – the curse was gone, considerably raising its market value. We declined the offers and lived there happily for over twenty years, until moving to Jerusalem, in 1997.

Our three younger children married within ten months, beginning in 1981. Dena married Yonah Gewirtz, son of Rabbi Aaron and Edith Gewirtz. Our youngest daughter Sori married Moshe Teitelbaum, son of Avraham Yehoshua Heschel and Shula Teitelbaum. And our son Chaim Zvi married Esti Munk, daughter of Rabbi Yechezkel and Rochel Munk of Telshe Yeshiva in Cleveland. These were wonderful events, but needless to say they severely strained our finances. I borrowed a considerable sum to finance the weddings – painstakingly paying it off over the next few years. Our daughters and their husbands lived in Brooklyn and Queens, and then for a while in Monsey.

Miriam became a teacher, Dena an actuary, and Sori a paralegal. The primacy of family was a hallmark of our home and our upbringing; Jackie and I emphasized this value to our children during their formative years. (In my rabbinic experience, this value is more difficult to instill in young men than in young women, for the men's yeshivot often become the new "family," supplanting the biological nuclear one.) In a few years, we were blessed with beautiful and intelligent grandchildren (are there any other kind?), and the dream of seeing generations continue in our family was fulfilled.

Me with my daughter Dena and her family, the Gewirtzes

Miriam and Dena and their husbands now live in Indiana, Sori and her husband in Woodmere, New York, and Chaim Zvi and family in Monsey. As of this writing, the married grandchildren and their offspring, my great-grandchildren, live in Lakewood, Passaic (and elsewhere in New Jersey), Monsey, Queens, Los Angeles, Cincinnati, Cleveland, and St. Louis. Some still study in yeshivot in Jerusalem. In my generation one hardly even knew his grandparents, and now I have the pleasure of being a great-grandparent! How can one not be inordinately grateful for that blessing? Nor do I take for granted that our bonds with all our descendants remain strong and loving. I am deeply thankful for this blessing too.

A weekly Jewish history class that I began teaching in the late 1970s led to a new development in my life. Originally intended for the women of my *shul*, the class became very popular with ladies from all sectors of Monsey. In preparing these classes, I read a great deal, and Jewish history became almost an obsession. I thought to myself, "If only Jews knew their own story, how much more attached they would be to their heritage, traditions, and faith!" This idea germinated within me for quite a while. It was destined to play a very important role in my future.

After a few years of these women's classes, a number of men from the synagogue (in danger of being thought intellectually inferior to their wives) approached me to organize a class for them as well. I agreed, but stipulated that the men pay a registration fee of fifty dollars to either the synagogue or Shaarei Torah (the yeshiva I founded in 1977, to which the next chapter is dedicated). They agreed, and about thirty registered. (The women's class was free. No one seemed to notice this discrimination.) However, a number were physicians who couldn't attend the class regularly because of their professional schedules. One doctor asked if he could send his tape recorder to the class when he couldn't be there. Since he'd paid the registration fee, I could hardly refuse. The tapes proved most popular with his colleagues. Thus was born Rabbi Wein's history tape series.

Early in my Monsey career, I began speaking on behalf of many local and national institutions, and I soon became a regular on the Jewish lecture circuit. By the mid-1980s, I was pretty much a fixture. I spoke often in the New York area, and I was invited to almost every major and midsize Jewish community in the United States and Canada. I traveled from Portland, Maine, to Portland, Oregon, and from Miami and Houston to Minneapolis and Toronto. I spoke on behalf of yeshivot, synagogues, JCCs, Israel Bonds, Jewish Federations and many other charitable causes. I missed Jackie on these trips, short as they were, but her dedication to her fourth-grade students usually came first. When longer excursions were mandated, we found ways for her to accompany me to England, Scotland, Ireland, South Africa, Switzerland, and other countries. (In addition to broadening our horizons, these speaking engagements provided us with the supplemental income needed to reduce our wedding debts.)

Originally, I feared my congregants would resent my frequent trips. But I learned that a congregation is doubly proud of its rabbi if he is a national figure and a sought-after teacher and speaker. Somehow, the self-esteem of every congregant is enhanced. All in all, it became a win-win situation.

Moreover, I spoke to all segments of Orthodox Jewish society, escaping being pigeonholed. One year, I spoke at the annual convention of the OU, and the next night at that of Agudath Israel. The speeches were almost identical. The next week, I received phone calls from leading officers of each organization instructing me never again to speak for the other. I never again spoke for either organization in the United States, although I was invited to do so several times. (Nevertheless, my friendship with Rabbi Moshe Sherer, executive head of Agudath Israel, remained strong.)

As you can tell, I'm pretty disgusted with organized Jewish life and with people's obsessive interest in protecting their own turf rather than the welfare of the Jewish People. I believe Jewish life has ever been so. Still, ever since this OU-Aguda incident, I have attempted to stay away from organizations and Jewish politics. Somebody has to do it, but that somebody need not be me.

I've chosen other ways of trying to help the Jewish People globally. Given the increasing popularity of my taped lectures on Jewish history, I reasoned that a book on Jewish history from a traditional viewpoint would be an important addition to the Jewish bookshelf. While I was contemplating this venture, something strange occurred. On a trip to

Israel, I was walking in Jerusalem's Geula neighborhood when a man I didn't recognize approached me and asked, "Are you Berel Wein?" I answered in the affirmative. "What are you working on now?" he wanted to know. I answered that I had just completed two works in Hebrew on subjects in the Talmud. Published in Israel by Mossad HaRav Kook, both books sold out. I told my mysterious questioner that I was working on a third volume in that series. He retorted, "No, no, that's not what you should be doing. There are plenty of *kollel* students in Jerusalem who can do that. You should be writing history books for the Jewish People." He then disappeared into the crowd without identifying himself or even saying goodbye. Who was this person? Was I being sent a message from a Higher Source?

My idea for a history book coincided with the exponential growth of Mesorah Publications (ArtScroll), which in recent decades has become the primary teacher of the Jewish masses. Its founders and executive heads, Rabbis Meir Zlotowitz and Nosson Scherman, became friends of mine over the years. We never mixed business with pleasure, however, and were brutally honest with each other regarding publishing, book content, literary style, editing, and marketing.

There were and are practical sensitivities in the Orthodox Jewish world that I respected while writing my history books (and, in fact, this book as well). Nevertheless, I insisted on accuracy, not hagiography or propaganda. My first book, *Triumph of Survival*, covered more than three centuries of modern Jewish history, from 1648 onward. Mesorah published it under its newly created Shaar Press imprint, and it proved very successful. It has been reprinted several times and is even used as a textbook in many schools.

I wrote *Triumph of Survival* in longhand on a legal pad. My handwriting somewhat resembles my miserable singing voice, so Mesorah's transcribers had difficulty deciphering many of my immortal words. Envisioning further works of history from me, Rabbi Zlotowitz graciously presented me with a laptop and gave me rudimentary instructions on how to use it. He taught me that the two main buttons on the keyboard are "delete" and "save." His main instruction: "Always use the 'save' and 'delete' buttons wisely. Know when to use which button! Forget everything else."

Launching *Triumph of Survival* (Suffern, NY, 1990)

Thus, I entered the computer age, where I have operated for a quarter of a century. I obtained an e-mail address and eventually a website. Since then I have attempted to keep up with the ever-changing technology. (As of this writing, I'm an avid iPad user.)

After *Triumph of Survival*, I wrote *Herald of Destiny*, covering the medieval era; *Echoes of Glory*, about the Classical Era; and smaller works of general Jewish interest. I completed my history series with *Faith & Fate: The Story of the Jews in the Twentieth Century*. All these works were published by Mesorah. The publisher was also kind enough to commission me to write a commentary on *Pirkei Avos* as well as a Haggadah, which were both well received.

I have dear friends living in London, Alfred and Sue Birnbaum. Years ago they introduced to me a friend and neighbor of theirs, Matthew Miller. In recent years, Matthew Miller resurfaced in my life when he moved to Jerusalem and became the proprietor and head of Koren Publishers, and its division Maggid Books. I submitted the manuscript of

Patterns in Jewish History to him and he agreed to publish it. Since then, Maggid Books has become a warm home to me and my later writings. I have published a number of books with them, yet Matthew and I have remained good friends throughout these years. The personal interest and care shown to me by him and Gila Fine, Maggid's editor-in-chief, have enriched my writing experience. Maggid's professionalism coupled with its encouragement, wise comments and advice, and generous spirit have allowed me to publish a number of what I consider to be valuable works during my years here in Jerusalem. I am truly fortunate to have been included in their roster of authors and friends.

I have greatly enjoyed the challenge of producing all these books, though writing is a lengthy and sometimes tedious task, even when all the research has been completed and one knows what he wishes to say. These books also provided me with much-needed income to meet our mounting family obligations and to finally discharge all our debts.

Throughout my years as a rabbi, I have written weekly essays based upon the Torah portion of the week. In addition, I have written a large book in Hebrew containing five essays on each weekly Torah reading. (As of this writing, the editing of this work is nearing completion, and I hope to see it published soon.) For the past sixteen years, I've also

Launching *The Legacy* with South Africa's Chief Rabbi Warren Goldstein (seated, right) and Matthew Miller and Gila Fine (standing) (Jerusalem, 2008)

published a newsletter ten times a year, titled "The Wein Press." That's an awful lot of writing – but I have always enjoyed writing and sharing my thoughts. It offers an extraordinary opportunity to provide information and influence others, which is really what the current rabbinate is all about, or should be all about – informing and influencing Jews in numerous ways and on all levels.

Over the years, I've learned not to judge, especially regarding the appearance of other Jews. For a good while, I taught a monthly lunch-hour class to Syrian Jews working in Manhattan's garment district. After class, we would pray *Minchah* together. These Jews, whose appearance belied their inner piety, conducted a *Minchah* service that lasted forty-five minutes, reciting every word out loud and with great concentration. They taught me how to pray, and how never to judge a Jew by his looks.

I also taught evenings in Manhattan and Brooklyn. Driving into New York was very tiring, and I sometimes felt I might fall asleep at the wheel. So I always tried to find someone to accompany me, hoping the conversation would keep me alert. One night, I was forced to drive into the city alone. As I approached the entrance to the Thruway, I noticed a Hasid hitching a ride to the city. I gladly picked him up. To my disappointment, however, he didn't say a word. After twenty minutes, I began taking measures to stay awake. I opened the window to the cold air and turned on the radio. Out of respect for my companion, rather than listening to the hockey game or the news, I tuned to the classical music station. After a few moments, he said, "Isn't that Mahler's Fifth Symphony?" Well, that broke the ice, and we went on to have a fascinating conversation covering philosophy, history, current Jewish events, different streams of *Hasidut*, the yeshiva world, and more.

When I was about to deliver him to his destination, he thanked me for the ride and asked, "Where do you live?" I told him I lived in Monsey, up the hill. "And in what synagogue do you pray?" he queried. I answered that I attended Bais Torah. "Isn't that Rabbi Wein's *shul*?" he noted. I confirmed that I prayed with Rabbi Wein regularly. Then he replied, "Judging by our conversation, if Rabbi Wein has people of your caliber in that synagogue, it must be really hard for him to speak regularly to such an astute audience."

"You have no idea how difficult it is for Rabbi Wein to speak every Shabbat in that synagogue!" I confirmed. I bade him adieu, realizing once again that you cannot and should not judge by externals.

Tough as it was to keep up with that "astute audience," I served as the rabbi of Bais Torah for twenty-four years, until 1997. Since the late 1980s, Jackie and I visited Israel every summer, and we decided to move there as soon as we could. Beginning in 1992, we spent two to three months a year in Israel. Our apartment was then ready and we slowly furnished it, making official *aliyah* in 1994. I informed my congregation that I would be moving to Jerusalem by the end of the summer of 1997.

I found it very hard to leave such wonderful people and dear friends, but Jerusalem took precedence in our hearts. (My father had moved to Monsey in 1982 and spent Shabbat and holidays with us. He was a fixture in the synagogue. Yet he also made *aliyah* with us, though he was almost ninety.) Monsey was a special place for my family, and we left it with fond memories and a bittersweet feeling. We sold our home, paid off all our debts, and registered to receive Social Security. So ended the Monsey chapter of our lives. I have returned to Monsey and to Bais Torah numerous times since, and while it's always a pleasure to reunite with old friends, it is perpetually invigorating to return home to Jerusalem.

I believe I left Bais Torah at the right time and under the right circumstances. A rabbi should never overstay his welcome or outlive his usefulness. Like a good guest, he must know when to leave.

Chapter 10

Building Shaarei Torah: A Labor of Love

"For the last sixty years, I have taught Torah somehow, somewhere, almost every day."

One of my dreams was to found a yeshiva that would train young Torah scholars and Jewish leaders. I imagine that I was subconsciously trying to emulate my beloved grandfather, Rabbi Chaim Zvi Rubinstein, who created such an institution in Chicago after World War I. When I left the OU and helped found and build Congregation Bais Torah in Monsey, I also founded (in 1977) Yeshiva Shaarei Torah, a yeshiva high school including a post-high-school *beit midrash* program and a rigorous track that led to rabbinic ordination. In retrospect, this project was overly ambitious, but somehow the school ran well for twenty years. Many hundreds of students studied in the yeshiva, and it produced numerous successful and distinguished rabbis, educators, and community leaders. At the end of the nineteenth century, my grandfather had founded a yeshiva in Jaffa called Shaarei Torah; I merely appropriated the name and planted it in Suffern. But it didn't take root right away. In fact, it almost didn't get there at all.

In 1973, while still at the OU, I met the legendary philanthropist Zev Wolfson. For almost forty years, we had a superb and mutually productive relationship. I helped him with several educational projects he sponsored in Israel. We exchanged ideas about Judaism in America as well. He told me he had a guarantee from Rabbi Aaron Kotler that if he devoted himself to building Torah in America and Israel, he would succeed in business. That guarantee was redeemed in full.

One of Wolfson's projects was to build yeshivot in America, which would eventually stand on their own financially and otherwise. Some did; others failed and closed. He originally partnered with Rabbi Henoch Leibowitz, *rosh yeshiva* of Chofetz Chaim Yeshiva in Queens; the Chofetz Chaim branches throughout America were established largely through their help. Wolfson also helped Rabbi Shlomo Riskin of Lincoln Square Synagogue open his multifaceted educational institutions in America (before he moved to Israel – to become rabbi of Efrat – and founded an enormous complex of educational and service institutions).[1]

Wolfson had a foundation based in Israel that was somehow affiliated with the Jewish Agency and other quasi-official government bodies. It allocated considerable sums to the creation of Diaspora high schools that would strengthen students' ties with Judaism and Israel. I discussed my idea for a yeshiva high school with him, and he agreed to help. In my mind, Yeshiva Shaarei Torah of Rockland was born as soon as I left the OU.

It was almost stillborn. There were myriad delicate details to be dealt with before Shaarei Torah opened in September 1977. First we needed a location. There was an empty school building in Orangeburg, near Monsey. I intended to open the school outside Monsey, correctly assessing that the yeshiva high schools in town would resent my opening a competing institution on their turf. The Orangeburg building was put up for bidding – with a five-year lease offered by the school board – and I won. Thanks to Wolfson's seed money, I met the board's financial requirements.[2]

---

1. It was through Zev Wolfson that I came to know Rabbi Riskin, and our long relationship has transcended some of our ideological differences. I consider him among the great builders of Torah and Orthodoxy in our generation.
2. Lest Yeshiva Shaarei Torah sound too sectarian for Wolfson's Israeli organization, the official name was the Orangetown-Monsey Hebrew School. Yeshiva Shaarei Torah was listed on official documents as a project of said school.

However, the board had to hold a public meeting to finalize the deal, and that meeting was a disaster for the yeshiva. As one leader of the opposition so elegantly put it, "There's no room at the inn for you people." A lot of open anti-Semitism was expressed, and sadly, many of our most vociferous and malicious opponents were Jews. A few brave people – all non-Jews – defended the yeshiva's right to lease the property, but to no avail. The board backed out of the lease, and I was forced to look for a building in Monsey.

The local school board put a large building in Monsey up for lease. The building was far too big for my thirty-five students, but it had a kitchen, lunchroom, gymnasium, and library. September was fast approaching, so I took the plunge. I assembled a faculty of yeshiva graduates with teaching experience. An excellent general studies principal and several dedicated teachers of English, math, and science completed my staff. And I embarked upon twenty years of daily fundraising for the yeshiva. Everyone may wish to become a *rosh yeshiva*, but today the *rosh yeshiva* must be a constant fundraiser, and not everyone wants to be that (and not everyone can).

I was determined that the yeshiva pay a living wage and provide its staff with term life insurance and health insurance, aside from more minor benefits. The yoke of fundraising was oppressive, and many times I felt like giving up. But somehow I kept going, despite terrible periods when the faculty was owed months of salary and I couldn't look these people in the eye.

In tough times, I was always strengthened and gratified that many members of the OU's lay commissions sent their children and grandchildren to Shaarei Torah. It was a much-needed vote of confidence. Miraculously, the yeshiva always pulled itself out of debt and keep functioning. I made yearly visits to other communities near and far in search of financial aid. Though the burden was heavy, our students' accomplishments were heartening and gave me the strength to continue.

Fundraising may not be fun, but sometimes it can be funny. I once asked a wealthy person for a sizable donation, certain he would give it to me because I had helped him out of a difficult situation. He gave me a check with a flourish, but it was one zero less than the sum I had expected. My face must have registered disappointment, because he told me, "Rabbi, don't worry so much. God will help." In my frustration, I snapped, "'God will help' is *my* speech to people, not yours. You should write a bigger check and leave God out of it." Shocked by my own brazenness, I apologized – and he, in turn, added the requisite zero.

Fundraising can also be inspiring. There was another Shaarei Torah in the New York area. In response to a pre-Pesach mail campaign, we once received a check for $5,000 from someone who regularly donated $50. I had the secretary call him and ask whether he'd stuffed the wrong check into the envelope. He acknowledged the error but said, "Keep the check and deposit it. I'll make it up to the other institution. It appears that God wanted you to have this money." And there were always unsolicited surprise donations. The randomness of fundraising strengthened my belief in God's guiding hand in human affairs. Over the twenty years that I headed Shaarei Torah, well over $30 million was raised on behalf of the yeshiva. I still don't know how that happened.

Marketing my history tapes was a major venture for Shaarei Torah, as all the income from the tapes went directly to the yeshiva. Staff members duplicated, packed, and shipped tapes to fill the orders that kept coming in.

I was truly gratified by the incredible response to my tapes. I had avid listeners in the Hasidic community (I believe I was underground entertainment in Monroe and Williamsburg), within the Reform movement, and even among the unaffiliated. I received letters from people who had been totally non-observant, thanking me for helping them find their way back to synagogue life and meaningful Judaism. I even had listeners in prison.

I discovered that Jewish history was a fascinating though much neglected field throughout the Jewish world. Increasingly, I realized that knowledge of Jewish history, if presented traditionally but popularly, could boost faith and observance tremendously. This subject was too important to be left to the academicians. So I began devoting my spare time – late at night and very early in the morning – to writing history books. Because of the popularity of the tapes (and later, books), I was offered many more speaking engagements than I would have received otherwise. I saw that blessing as an indirect reward for channeling the income from the tapes into our yeshiva.

I continued recording lectures, and these cassettes were also distributed through the yeshiva. Some people bought every one. I was proud to have been one of the main originators of taped lectures for the Jewish market. (Quite a few non-Jews bought my tapes too!) I helped create a genre of Torah study that today is mainstream and extremely well-developed via CDs, DVDs, MP3 players, iPods, and other infernal devices. The Jewish world's best minds have allowed their thoughts to be heard worldwide for the immense benefit of Jews everywhere.

Maybe it's my distinctive Chicago accent, but I'm regularly greeted by strangers who've heard one of my recorded lectures. I can be at a restaurant or an airport ticket counter and just utter a few words, and people come up to me and say they've listen to my tapes. At Victoria Falls in Zimbabwe, I was walking in the rain forest, a few meters from the statue of David Livingstone (the "lost" explorer and English missionary of nineteenth-century fame). After hearing me say a few words to my wife, a Jew from Brooklyn approached me and said, "Rabbi Wein, I presume!" Ah, fame does pursue those worthy of it.

Our school building was torched by an arsonist one Saturday night. I was sickened that as the fire department attempted to extinguish the flames, a large crowd of non-Jews gathered, shouting, "Burn, baby, burn!" This callous, casual, open anti-Semitism is not as rare in America as Jews would like to believe. And this occurred in the holy city of Monsey, regarded by many Jews living there as a secure bastion of Jewish life, free of bigotry.

One-third of the building was destroyed, and the case was never solved. The yeshiva soldiered on, despite the lingering smell of smoke and the hardships inflicted by the fire. Yet it was clear to me that Shaarei Torah needed its own building, in a Jewish neighborhood, rather than renting on the border of a hostile, non-Jewish district.

As the end of our lease with the school board approached, I began raising money for a proper yeshiva building. I convinced both Wolfson and Avner Yisraeli, the wonderful representative of the former's Israeli-based arm, of this imperative, and the organization gave us a sizable grant. Congregation Bais Torah, for its part, was kind enough to lease (for ninety-nine years, at a rent of one dollar per year) a large plot of land adjacent to the synagogue for the yeshiva to build upon.

I ordered a cornerstone made of Jerusalem stone, and my beloved friends Jacob and Belle Rosenbaum dedicated it. As mentioned, we were honored to have Rabbi Yaakov Kamenetsky attend the cornerstone laying. Overcoming many zoning, financial, legal, and construction difficulties, the building of the yeshiva was completed in 1983.

At long last, I went to Ramapo Town Hall to receive the certificate of occupancy for the new building. The clerk searched his files but found no document prepared for Shaarei Torah. I almost wept with frustration, for the legal and zoning problems we had surmounted were already legendary. I asked him to look again, but no luck. In desperation, I suddenly recalled that the application for the certificate had been filed in the name of Bais Torah, since the yeshiva building was on synagogue property. The clerk searched the file cabinet once more, looking for Bais Torah this time. He returned triumphantly and handed me the precious document to me. "Well," he said, "at least it's the same last name [Torah] for both institutions."

I couldn't help thinking, "What a wise comment! If only we Jews would think that way – that it's the same 'last name,' Torah, we all strive for – how different our society would look and behave!"

Laying the cornerstone (Suffern, NY, 1983)

The yeshiva flourished in its new quarters. Yisraeli visited often, and we became good friends. He was an old-fashioned non-observant Jew, a species now extinct. Originally from Vilna, he had a soft spot for Jewish observance and Torah. He would stand in the yeshiva's large study hall, watching the students at *Minchah* prayers. He didn't participate, but afterward he would compliment me on how well the services were conducted and on the sincerity of the students.

Several times, financial scandal threatened other American educational institutions supported by Wolfson's Israeli branch. I was the point man for both him and Yisraeli, averting this potentially lethal danger and, even worse, its publication. I even flew to Israel once, arriving in the morning and leaving that same evening, to straighten out a very volatile situation regarding the sale of property belonging to a school that was closing. The proceeds were to revert to the Israeli organization, but somehow a sizable amount had been deducted by the heads of the school for settlement payments to certain teachers. I raised sufficient funds to return the difference to the foundation, thus salvaging Wolfson and Yisraeli's relationship with their other schools.

As I grew more involved with Yisraeli, I often asked myself, "How has this Jew been privileged to help support so many Torah institutions?" I thought about his youth in Vilna in the 1920s. At that time, Rabbi Chaim Ozer Grodzensky was the acknowledged head of Lithuanian religious Jewry and he lived in Vilna. Through his contacts with rabbis in America and elsewhere, he acquired enormous support for the city's yeshivot. He was a great Torah scholar and a moral model for his generation. I once heard from my teachers that the Chofetz Chaim's piety masked his tremendous scholarship and intellectual greatness, while Reb Chaim Ozer's scholarship and intellectual greatness masked his piety.

I asked Avner if in his youth he had ever met Rabbi Grodzensky. He told me the following story:

"I was the president of the Young Jewish Socialist League at the University of Vilna. One year, right after Purim, this bearded Jew wearing a caftan appeared on campus, looking for me. He told me he was Rabbi Grodzensky's secretary, and the rabbi would like me to visit him the next day at home. I couldn't imagine what the rabbi wanted, but I was curious, so I appeared at his home at the appointed time.

"Rabbi Grodzensky greeted me warmly. He proceeded to set out a tray of cookies and tea. 'Avner,' he said, 'listen to me pronounce the blessings, and you just say, "Amen." Then please eat something.' I did as he asked. Then he said to me, 'Pesach is approaching, and I want you to organize a proper *Seder* sponsored by your Socialist organization. Everyone attending should have four cups of wine and matzo.' He gave me a few hundred-dollar bills with which to purchase whatever I needed for such a *Seder*. Then he gently extended his hand and asked that I shake it as a sign that we'd made a deal regarding the *Seder*. I shook his hand and rose to leave, the money safely in my pocket.

"As I turned to say goodbye, he took a Polish postage stamp from his desk drawer and tore it in half. 'I had originally written you a letter requesting that you visit me,' he explained, 'but then I sent my secretary to find you personally. Perhaps I owe the Polish government the postage stamp to which it otherwise would have been entitled.'

"I organized a *Seder* on campus for three hundred Jewish students. And that's how I met Rabbi Chaim Ozer Grodzensky."

I now realized that Yisraeli's support for the American yeshivot was really Rabbi Grodzensky's doing.

I was in Israel when Avner Yisraeli passed away. He had asked his family to make certain that I eulogized him at his funeral, which I did – with tears in my eyes, a somewhat shaky voice, and uncertain Hebrew vocabulary.

I consulted Rabbi Kamenetsky on yeshiva matters and he gave me critical guidelines for running the school. He said, "A yeshiva should include, not exclude. Only for pornography and theft are you allowed to expel a student. Otherwise you must hold on to students at almost all costs. As the Talmud instructs us, push away with your left hand, but draw near with your right. And a yeshiva is not a 'Sodom bed.' [In Sodom they had a bed that was one-size-fits-all: The tall person was cut down to fit it, and the short person was stretched.] Leave room for individuality, and don't insist on rigid conformity. Especially nurture the mischievous ones. Rabbi Chaim Ozer Grodzensky was expelled from *cheder* for riding a goat into the room! And look how he turned out!"

In all the years I headed Shaarei Torah, very few students were expelled. My faculty often complained about my disciplinary leniencies, and though I sympathized with these colleagues – after all, they were in the trenches – I mainly upheld my policies. Decades later, I still feel I was correct, especially seeing how wonderfully the graduates of Shaarei Torah turned out – particularly the troublemakers!

Rabbi Kamenetsky once rescued Shaarei Torah and me from defamation. One day, four distinguished rabbis from "down the hill" in Monsey came to advise me to close down Shaarei Torah, because it taught secular studies. I had no right to call it a yeshiva, they said, and Monsey had sufficient yeshiva high schools without it. I was taken aback. I pointed out to them that the yeshiva high school that they apparently championed also offered secular studies. They claimed to be shocked by this revelation. I saw immediately that this visit was just a power squeeze by one of the four, a well-known religious vigilante, and that the other three were just along for the ride. I politely ushered them out of my office and thanked them for their concern.

Three weeks later, the zealot mailed out 4,000 letters – to virtually every Jewish home in Monsey – defaming me and the yeshiva in Chicago where I had studied, denouncing Shaarei Torah, and declaring that I had no standing or right to head any yeshiva, and that no one should support Shaarei Torah or send his children there. I have never fathomed what ticked this man off about Shaarei Torah or about me, since I had never met him. Perhaps Shaarei Torah was too successful, and he perceived some threat to his constituency's hegemony in Monsey. In any event, I ignored the matter, simply stating the facts as written here to my congregants in Bais Torah. I was deeply hurt, as was my wife, but we kept our poise and peace and went about our business.

My colleagues at Shaarei Torah were incensed, however, and determined to fight back. They visited Rabbi Kamenetsky, who thereupon wrote a strong defense of Shaarei Torah and me, and condemned the zealot. Rabbi Kamenetsky's statement was sent out to the same Monsey mailing list that had received the letter. The zealot called Rabbi Kamenetsky to explain, but Rabbi Kamenetsky simply said, "Now you call me? Why didn't you call before you sent out your letter?"

The matter soon faded away, though Shaarei Torah's reputation was damaged.

A few months later, I met the perpetrator in our local bank. "I hope you realize I meant nothing personal," he said. I just stared at him, then smiled and walked away. I would hate to see how a "personal" vendetta of his looked.

After a decade of living alone in Chicago since my mother's death, caring for his small congregation in the East Rogers Park neighborhood, my father agreed to move to Monsey. He was blessed with remarkably good health for a man his age, and our family was delighted to have him around. Originally he lived in an apartment near my synagogue, but after my son became part of the yeshiva faculty and bought a home in Monsey, my father moved in with him and his family. He taught his great-grandchildren the Hebrew alphabet, just as he had taught those holy letters to me decades earlier.

The yeshiva and the synagogue became my father's home. He learned regularly with many members of the *shul*, and everyone respected him. He spent four hours a day at the yeshiva, learning with anyone who needed his guidance, whether it was a ninth-grader or a rabbinical student. His mere presence – quiet, unassuming, serene – inspired faculty and students alike.

In the twenty years I headed Shaarei Torah, I taught every student there: a daily fifteen-minute *Mussar* class before *Minchah*; Jewish history lessons to the high school; Friday-morning Talmud lectures to the seniors and older *semichah* students;[3] and a lecture on the weekly Torah reading to the entire student body on Friday before school dismissal.

For at least the last sixty years, I have taught Torah somehow, somewhere, almost every day. My father once told me that teaching Torah was "our family business." I am gratified that all my children have stayed in the "business."

The *semichah* curriculum at Shaarei Torah was thorough and wide-ranging and included written exams requiring independent research in the laws of *kashrut*, Shabbat and holidays, *mikvaot*, nid-

---

3. In preparing these Talmud classes, I stayed up very late Thursday nights. For a long period of my life, I required little sleep.

dah (family purity), *kiddushin* (marriage ceremony issues), and *aveilut* (mourning). In essence, the rabbinical student wrote an entire volume of *halachah* in taking these exams. This method departed from the oral exams of my yeshiva years. I've always considered orals a somewhat hit-or-miss affair, with many subjective factors entering into their administration. The thoroughness and difficulty of my law school and bar exams, both written, also influenced my decision to institute written *semichah* tests in Shaarei Torah. The standards for becoming a recognized Torah scholar and rabbi should certainly not be, God forbid, lower than for becoming an attorney. I spent many hours grading these exams.

I insisted that students write their answers in Hebrew. It is unthinkable that an aspiring rabbi be unable to read and write Hebrew fluently. Hebrew was the required foreign language in the Shaarei Torah high school. For most students, even after eight years of day school and yeshiva education, Hebrew was still quite "foreign."

A quasi-rabbinic internship program in my *shul* enabled quite a number of Shaarei Torah students (and faculty) to "practice." I am truly grateful to the long-suffering members of Bais Torah for allowing these young men to hone their speaking and teaching skills at congregants'

Me with the boys of Shaarei Torah

expense. Actually, some in the *shul* preferred these novices to their regular rabbi. I blithely ignored their assessments.

Shaarei Torah *semichah* was recognized by the Rabbinical Council of America as well as by the Chief Rabbinate of Israel. This "seal of approval" enabled some of our graduates to obtain prestigious rabbinic positions both in Israel and in North America.

Amid my synagogue duties, yeshiva responsibilities, speaking engagements, and history books, I nevertheless undertook heading and teaching at the *Mercaz L'Hachsharat Morim*/Teacher Training Institute, then in Brooklyn. I did so at the behest of Zev Wolfson and his Israeli organization, which financed much of the institute. The real heads were Rabbis Yoel Kramer and Hillel Mandel, Avi Shulman, and my son, Chaim. The objective was to train young Torah scholars in educational methods that would make them effective teachers. They would then be placed in day schools and yeshivot around the country, and even around the world. Despite the punishing commute to and from Brooklyn, I taught one night a week for twelve years.

Many students obtained degrees in special education and other fields associated with teaching and educational administration. Thanks to these degrees, from recognized universities, our graduates were in great demand. The student body spanned the entire Orthodox spectrum – yeshiva students, Hasidic, Centrist Orthodox, Zionist, and non-Zionist. Everyone found a place – and many a lifelong career and holy mission. Hundreds of young men have studied at the institute, and though not all became teachers, all were greatly enriched. The institute is one of the unsung heroes of Jewish education. It still functions today, effective and unassuming.

The board of directors of my alma mater yeshiva, Beis Medrash L'Torah/ Hebrew Theological College (by then located in Skokie), asked me to become its president. I had a strong emotional pull to consider it. I dreamt that Skokie could produce the rabbinic and educational leadership necessary for the growth of Orthodoxy in America (and in Israel as well). And my grandfather would certainly have been proud that his grandson was heading the yeshiva he had founded sixty-five years earlier.

But I couldn't accept the offer. If fundraising for Shaarei Torah was burdensome, raising money for the yeshiva in Skokie would be ten times more so. The administrative and fundraising duties would prevent me from doing any meaningful teaching in the yeshiva; instead, I would be only a distant influence. In addition, Jackie and I were looking forward to moving to Jerusalem, whereas Skokie understandably wanted a long-term commitment. These and other personal reasons militated against my accepting the position. So I stayed in Monsey for the next decade.[4]

As mentioned, Mossad HaRav Kook published two volumes of my Talmudic discourses, culled from many of my Friday-morning Talmud lectures at Shaarei Torah. My devoted student and friend Harel Kohen also organized and annotated a considerable number of my lectures relating to the months of Elul and Tishrei, which appeared in a Hebrew volume. Naturally, I am gratified that my modest efforts in Torah have seen publication.

I doubt I would have produced them if not for my teaching and lecturing duties at the yeshiva. (When I began writing and publishing on Jewish history, I felt I could no longer do justice to producing works on Talmudic subjects in Hebrew, except for my occasional Shabbat Hagadol and Shabbat Shuva lectures and some other works written for family occasions.) An apocryphal story is told about the head of a yeshiva who delivered a lecture based on his complicated interpretation of a passage in the Talmud. He was later asked what source compelled him to come up with such an ingenious explanation. He replied: "I had to deliver a lecture!" When one is committed to delivering a lecture, the creative mind works wondrously to develop new ideas and insights. Perhaps that's why the rabbis of the Talmud (Taanit 7a) said, "I learned most from my students." Having students demands study and creativity. Thus, I am most grateful to have headed Shaarei Torah for twenty years.

---

4. Twenty years later, one of the lay directors of the Skokie yeshiva offhandedly asked if I was interested in becoming the *rosh yeshiva*, a position that had recently become vacant. I was firmly settled in Jerusalem by then. In any event, I doubted I was right for the job. But I was flattered to be considered for such a position of Torah leadership.

Shaarei Torah has produced quite a few outstanding figures. Among its graduates in Israel and the Diaspora are noted rabbis, heads of yeshivot and *kollelim*, physicians, attorneys, successful entrepreneurs, professors in leading universities, teachers, educational administrators and executives, prominent outreach specialists, and many active lay leaders in diverse communities. My teachers in yeshiva in Chicago likened the Jewish People to an army: Just as an army has many different units, each with its own task – artillery, infantry, tanks, intelligence, supply, etc. – so too the Jewish world requires scholars, lay people, entrepreneurs, professionals, etc. All these "units" are necessary for our success and survival as a vital and eternal people. To me, Shaarei Torah embodied this most practical educational principle, allowing the student to find his place within Jewish society. I'm exceptionally proud of Shaarei Torah's graduates: the diversity of their achievements reflects the yeshiva's philosophy that a broad spectrum of people, life missions, and beneficial activities all can thrive under the protective umbrella of Torah and observance.

Unfortunately, today this type of yeshiva is something of an anomaly. Though the problem of "youth at risk" will always be with us – as it always has been – a one-size-fits-all system of Jewish education certainly exacerbates the problem. King Solomon advised us to "educate the youngster according to *his* path." Not everyone has the same path. Square pegs should not be hammered into round holes in order to fit a preconceived ideal of the Jewish world. Rabbi Kamenetsky was right about "nurturing the mischievous." Many are born leaders and become successful products of the yeshiva.

All over the world, Shaarei Torah graduates face the challenge of finding a proper yeshiva high school for their own sons. "If only we had a Shaarei Torah here!" they've told me. I am both flattered and saddened to hear that.

Chapter 11

A Lifelong Dream
Becomes Reality

"Just living in the Jewish state is exciting."

As I approached my sixtieth birthday, I began seriously planning my retirement years. Jackie and I both wanted to move to Israel. I had visited every year since 1989, including during the 1991 Gulf War. Though the war was deadly serious, it had a lighter, typically Israeli side as well. When I arrived at Ben-Gurion Airport, there was a large table piled with gas masks that were being issued to visitors. As I was given my mask, I noticed the Hebrew word *posul* – "invalid" – written on the box in large, red letters. I immediately told the clerk he'd given me a worthless gas mask. He looked at me in my black hat and gray beard and said, "I assure you, the mask is kosher *l'mehadrin min hamehadrin [strictly kosher]*." I meekly took the box back. I soon had occasion to wear that contraption during a Scud attack. The missile hit many miles away from my sealed room. Thank God, Saddam Hussein never used gas in those attacks: I could neither prove nor disprove the clerk's assessment of my gas mask.

Our comfortable apartment in Jerusalem, built by Manny Finkel, was ready for occupancy in the early 1990s. For several years before making *aliyah*, we spent much of our summers in Jerusalem, settling in to our apartment and attempting to become more Israeli. We had practically finished furnishing the place when we went to a store on Rehov Yaffo (Jaffa Road) to order carpeting for one of the bedrooms. A fine Jew sat in the store reciting Psalms. He took our order, and the carpeting was delivered and installed to our satisfaction. I paid him from my new Israeli checking account. The next summer, when we again spent two months in Jerusalem, we decided to carpet the other bedroom as well. We went to the same carpet store. The proprietor was again sitting and reciting Psalms. When he saw me, he bolted out of his chair and exclaimed, "Rabbi Wein, I was looking for you all year! Where were you?" I explained that I still spent most of the year in the United States, and asked why he needed me so desperately. He took from his wallet a fifty-shekel note wrapped within a piece of paper bearing my name. Apparently, upon reviewing last year's accounts, he had concluded that he'd overcharged me by fifty shekels; so he'd kept the money in his wallet the whole year, awaiting my return. Such incidents restore one's faith in honesty, goodness, and humanity.

When we visited the *aliyah* office in Manhattan to complete all the necessary paperwork, the Jewish Agency representative looked at us and uttered the immortal greeting given to all those naive Americans wanting to live in the Land of Israel: "Are you crazy?" We had been warned by others who had made *aliyah* that Israeli officials tended to be less than cheerful and forthcoming, but I was still shocked by the fellow's attitude.[1] Eventually, in 1994, all was in order and we officially became citizens of the Jewish state. We had fulfilled the Jewish dream of the ages in a very personal way.

Using my *aliyah* benefits, I purchased a car and embarked upon the harrowing experience of driving on Israeli roads. "Drive defensively" is certainly the motto of driving in Israel. Years of driving in New York City helped me prepare for the Israeli adventure. To obtain an Israeli driver's license, I had to take a private driving course, an extortion I considered unfair. I had driven for decades without incident! Nevertheless, I dutifully took the course. Certificate in hand, I showed up for

---

1. Since then, the great Nefesh B'Nefesh organization has simplified the *aliyah* process and made it very user-friendly. The result has been a vast increase in *aliyah*, with an exceptionally high rate of successful adaptation to living in Israel.

my driving test. The tester had me drive around the industrial section of Jerusalem's Talpiot neighborhood. Though this area is usually full of trucks, double parking, and horn honking, there was no traffic that day. The tester therefore wasn't sure my test was valid. I quoted him Rashi's comment that Noah might have been even more righteous had he lived in Avraham's generation. Thus, I told the tester, since he'd seen how well I'd driven with no traffic, he should simply imagine how well I would have done had there been more cars on the streets. He smiled, and I passed (though many Americans fail their first attempt). Only in Israel can one pass a driving test with Rashi's help.

Another insight emerged from this unlikely scenario. During the test, the tester is not allowed to reveal the results, yet he did tell me I was a good driver. I asked him what had so impressed him. He replied: "Before you pulled out of the space, you looked first in the rearview mirror to make sure there was no oncoming traffic. No one in Israel does that!" This is precisely the problem with much of Israeli life – no one looks in the rearview mirror of Jewish history and tradition. Many think the Jewish world began in 1897 or 1948 or 1967 or 1991. Thus, we just pull out into the traffic of our present and future circumstances, sometimes with disastrous results.

It was well known that we planned to move to Jerusalem by the summer of 1997. I began receiving job offers from Israeli institutions. Most of these positions involved substantial fundraising, so I politely declined. However, Rabbi Nota Schiller, head of Yeshivat Ohr Somayach in Jerusalem, visited my home in Monsey and offered me only teaching. Ohr Somayach's then fledgling Center Program enrolled young men who had completed college or graduate school (or had nearly done so) for one to two years of intensive Torah studies before they returned home to take up their careers. Teaching Talmud and history in such a program appealed to me, and I agreed to join the faculty.

I taught in that program for ten years and found the experience most challenging and satisfying. The students were tremendously motivated, intelligent, worldly, inquisitive, and determined to become Talmudic scholars relatively fast. My father had joined us on *aliyah*, and every day I brought him to my Talmud class at Ohr Somayach. It was a thrilling gift to teach Torah to these wonderful young men and have my father witness it.

The students came from South Africa, Canada, England, Australia, and the United States. They had all studied at prestigious universities, and each had a fascinating, almost unbelievable story of how he had been plucked from a completely secular background and deposited at Ohr Somayach. Many were Shabbat guests in our home, giving me the opportunity to learn more about their backgrounds and what epiphanies brought them to study Torah in Jerusalem. Many have remained friends, and even rabbinic colleagues, ever since.

One student had studied in a very large, liberal university in America. His family was completely non-observant but attended Rosh Hashanah services at a Reform temple, where the officiating clergy was a lesbian known for her radical ideas. During the service, she made an impassioned fundraising appeal for an environmental group fighting timber companies to save a California redwood forest. To buttress her case, she read a poem attributed to a long-departed Native American chief that extolled the various gods and spirits living in those majestic trees. It was like a course in paganism. My student told me, "Whatever that was all about, I knew it wasn't Judaism! I became determined to find out what Judaism is really all about. What an irony that a radical Reform lesbian rabbi sent me to Jerusalem to study Torah." I responded in the words of our rabbis, "The Lord has many messengers in this world."

And so He does. Most of my students at Ohr Somayach had similar stories, though perhaps less dramatic. The Lord is busy, so to speak, sorting out souls for good or for better.

At Ohr Somayach, I also taught a weekly class in Jewish history, as well as in rabbinics, as part of the Ohr LaGolah program. This program trains young *kollel* men to serve in Diaspora communities as teachers and rabbis. I enjoyed teaching these classes. The students knew almost nothing of Jewish history, or of what awaited them in working with assimilated Diaspora communities. To a certain extent, my task was to open their eyes and minds, playing devil's advocate regarding certain outlooks they had formed in their sheltered yeshiva years. The classes were so successful that outsiders also started to attend, and students recorded the lectures for their wives and friends.

A few students were shocked by the facts of Jewish history that contradicted the legends, myths, and worldview in which they had been indoctrinated. They reported me to the powers that be at Ohr Somayach as a heretic. But eventually, somewhat grudgingly, even these students understood my purposes. Teaching at Ohr Somayach was really a sheer pleasure. Many of my students are now Jewish leaders worldwide. I'm immensely proud of their accomplishments in the Jewish world they've built through their influence and example.

After moving to Jerusalem, I sought to realize a second lifelong dream: to fulfill the commandment of writing a Torah scroll. My wife and I commissioned the writing of a *sefer Torah* dedicated to the honor, memory, and appreciation of our parents. It took a number of years to be completed, whereupon we held a gala celebration at Ohr Somayach. (We loaned the Torah to the yeshiva for its regular use.) This event was especially moving and meaningful for us. Both my lifelong hopes – living in Jerusalem and writing a *sefer Torah* – had been accomplished. Numerous people participated in the Torah dedication – friends, members of my synagogue, and perhaps most important, my students from the Center Program. Many of them told me how much they appreciated the ceremony, and hoped they too would be able to replicate the experience.

Due to my background as a lawyer, OU kashrut administrator, rabbi, and *rosh yeshiva*, many students saw me not only as a teacher but as someone who had successfully negotiated the churning waters of modern and professional life. Somehow that gave them greater confidence in their abilities to do the same when they left the Center Program and returned to their homes and their academic and professional pursuits. When their non-observant parents visited them in Jerusalem, they often brought them to my class. They told me they wanted to show them that Judaism was relevant and meaningful; that observing the commandments and values of Judaism and studying Torah was normal, not anachronistic or foreign.

Naturally, I was delighted to help. Returning to Jewish observance in a family that for generations was non-observant is intellectually and emotionally wrenching. Helping people accomplish this difficult goal is not only an experience of faith and theology; it is primarily an act of compassion and understanding.

Our apartment is located in the Jerusalem neighborhood of Rechavia. Back in 1993, when my wife and I started coming to Israel every summer, I attended daily services at the Gra Synagogue in the adjacent Shaarei Chesed neighborhood. On Shabbat, I would attend Beit Knesset HaNasi (The President's Synagogue), built in the 1930s and so called because two presidents of Israel prayed there. The *shul* had attracted distinguished people over the years, including Rabbis Isaac Halevi Herzog and Nissan Zaks, Chief Justice Menachem Elon, and two presidents of Israel, Yitzchak Ben-Zvi and Zalman Shazar. In the 1990s, Rechavia and that synagogue were undergoing a distinct demographic change. More religious, English-speaking Jews were moving into the neighborhood, until then a bastion of secular German Jews. The synagogue's membership was rapidly declining, ravaged by age and time, and there was no official rabbi (though there were several unofficial ones).

Some of the newly arrived Americans and British joined the synagogue, chief among them my old friend Reuven Davidman (whom I knew from New York), as well as a young lawyer whose wife's relatives were friends, neighbors, and worshipers in my synagogue in Monsey. They proposed that during my six-week summertime stay I give a sermon Shabbat morning, a class Shabbat afternoon in English, as well as a history lecture during the week – all in the hope that my involvement would attract the growing number of English-speaking residents of Rechavia and Shaarei Chesed to join the synagogue. I made it clear to them that I had no aspirations to be a pulpit rabbi in Jerusalem, but I agreed to speak and teach as they'd requested. I spoke after the morning services had ended, in order to allow the Israelis – and anyone else who wished – to escape before I began. I enjoyed the experience and even occasionally, very occasionally, spoke in Hebrew.

More and more people came to hear me speak, and the synagogue and I agreed that when I settled in the neighborhood permanently, this schedule of speaking, teaching, and lecturing would continue. There was no discussion of my becoming the official rabbi, though Reuven insisted that it was only a matter of time. So with both Beit Knesset HaNasi and Yeshivat Ohr Somayach in my future, I no longer looked at my move to Jerusalem as "retiring."

After several years as the unofficial rabbi of Beit Knesset HaNasi, I was elected the official one. I added a Friday-morning Torah class, which also proved popular, as well as two Talmud classes. I had the distinct honor and pleasure of meeting the venerable scholar and *rav* of Shaarei Chesed, Rabbi Avraham David Rosenthal. I had numerous conversations with him on Torah subjects, and he enlightened me regarding certain customs that were prevalent in Jerusalem, especially in our adjoining neighborhoods. He and I exchanged books we had authored, and he was a wise and kind mentor to me in many matters. I referred all major halachic issues to him for his decision. He never answered a *kashrut* question by stating, "It's kosher," or "It's *treif.*" Rather, he would say, "It is acceptable," or "It is not fitting for you." After his passing, his son became the *rav* of Shaarei Chesed. By then I was the rabbi at Beit Knesset HaNasi and no longer prayed in Shaarei Chesed, so I didn't have the opportunity to establish as strong a relationship with the son as I had with the father.

I began teaching history one morning a week at a large senior citizens' *kollel* in the neighborhood. All in all, my plate was pretty full. Yet I found time to continue writing a number of works on the history of the Talmud and Mishnah, and on patterns in Jewish history; a large Hebrew volume containing five major essays on every *parshah* of the Torah; a book I coauthored with my friend Rabbi Warren Goldstein, chief rabbi

Teaching at Beit Knesset HaNasi

of South Africa, on Torah values as represented by Lithuanian Jewry; and two weekly articles, distributed through my website and synagogue, on the *parshah* of the week and on general Jewish subjects. My articles on Jewish issues appeared in the Friday *Jerusalem Post* for about a decade, before the paper put me out to pasture.

Writing is a taskmaster. If I don't always enjoy the process, I usually feel rewarded by the result. My *parshah* articles are circulated throughout the Jewish world and distributed in many synagogues. I receive numerous e-mails and letters about these pieces. (Some people still actually take paper and pen in hand and use the postal service!) Even when people have the temerity to disagree with my point of view, I appreciate their feedback. It provokes thought and analysis, and often a reconsideration of my opinions on matters of vital concern to the Jewish People.

I have received numerous comments from Conservative and Reform rabbis who object to my harsh, constant criticism of their distortion of Jewish values, their political correctness and faddishness. I sympathize with them, for they face terrible choices and a very difficult constituency. Yet they are destroying Jewish life and family in North America. I am saddened by the abject failure of the Reform and Conservative movements and their clergy to hold fast to any red lines of tradition. Apparently nothing is sacrosanct. But such are the risks of trying to keep your balance on a slippery slope. Eventually, everything traditional and genuine falls away, and society is left with a hodgepodge of pluralism, feminism, environmentalism, humanism, liberalism, universalism, pacifism – whatever "ism" is in vogue – passed off as Judaism. Justice Louis Dembitz Brandeis once wrote glowingly about his uncle, Louis Dembitz, an Orthodox Jew and prominent attorney in Kentucky. He describes his uncle's serene and beautiful Shabbat, then comments, "I long also for the serenity of such a Sabbath, but without its restrictions." And therein lies the crux of the matter. Without the restrictions, the serenity of the Sabbath disappears. The Conservative movement doomed itself by allowing its congregants to drive to synagogue on Shabbat. Sixty years later, Conservative synagogues are nearly empty on Shabbat, and most congregants experience no Sabbath serenity. Slogans about pluralism haven't prevented one intermarriage, just as raucous demonstrations and stone-throwing in protest of Shabbat desecration by *Charedi* zealots have not yet produced one Shabbat-observing Jew.

The Land of Israel is one of surpassing beauty and fascination. I loved our tours of the Galilee and the Golan with our visiting grandchildren. Perhaps in another incarnation I was a tour guide, because I enjoy the scenery and historical sites so much. To see the entire Bible come alive before one's eyes is emotionally and spiritually elevating. The battlefields of the Horns of Hittin outside Kibbutz Lavi, the Valley of Destruction in the Golan, and the fields surrounding Latrun also bring to life the history of modern Israel and its struggle for survival. Jackie and I could no longer keep up with our grandchildren's hiking and climbing, but in our own way we enjoyed the trips and excursions as much as they did.

After my years of constant traveling with the OU, I never thought I'd enjoy travel again. Nevertheless, after we came to Israel I got my second wind and actually learned to enjoy traveling. Because of my speaking engagements, we visited the United States, South Africa, England, Hong Kong, and Europe almost annually. We even traveled to Australia and New Zealand. We found wonderful friends in all these places, as well as family, and met many important personages in the Jewish world. Whoever said travel is broadening had it right.

Of course, I also enjoyed the fact that I would invariably meet people who had heard my lectures on tape or on Israeli cable TV. I was always amazed at the variety of these listeners and viewers. I again saw the wisdom of King Solomon's adage "Cast your bread upon the waters." In our generation, Torah must be spread by all possible means. One's words of Torah and Jewish knowledge may influence unseen others who may be worlds away, geographically and spiritually. One never knows.

I was in Israel during the Second Lebanon War and the Second Intifada. Standing on my porch, I could see tracer bullets being fired at the Jerusalem neighborhood of Gilo from the Arab village of Beit Jala. A bus blew up only two blocks from our home, and all our windows rattled. The Moment Café, also only two blocks from our building, was blown up by a suicide bomber one Saturday night. Jackie and I were walking home, fortunately coming from the direction farthest from the café. But we were shaken to see people fleeing the scene and ambulances stream-ing onto our street. I have also lived through the Gush Katif evacuation and the Lebanon pullout, both of which have proven very unwise. I was here for Operation Grapes of Wrath in the West Bank and Operation Cast Lead against Gaza. I have been a victim of the Goldstone Report and the continuing enmity and fecklessness of the Palestinians, the UN, the EU, and the elitist know-it-alls here in Israel and abroad who piously fan the flames of anti-Semitism and terror.

One thing I've learned from living in Israel through all these events is that the enemies of Israel, of Jews and of Judaism, target me as well. When they speak of the hated Jew, they mean me. I understood that concept intellectually during my decades of life in the United States. But now that I live in Israel, I know it in my bones – instinctively, vis-cerally, and emotionally. And in a certain way that has become a great comfort to me, a bond with past Jewish generations and an attachment to the Jewish story of the ages.

My years as a rabbi have taught me never to be overly enthusiastic about people, situations, or projects. Human beings are just that – only human. So I'm not especially disturbed by Israel's failings and social problems. Because of my lowered and realistic expectations, my absorp-tion into Israel has been relatively easy.

Early in my rabbinic career in the US, I felt that American Jewry was too organized, and consequently too competitive, too turf-conscious, with enormous duplication of efforts and waste of human and material resources. I always shied away from such Jewish organizations. Mov-ing to Israel, where there is an official rabbinate, competition among religious political parties, and enormous tensions and vindictiveness in religious matters, I was determined to remain uninvolved. I eschewed the standard Israeli rabbinic garb and have never attempted to be part of the official rabbinate (having learned from the many American rab-bis who tried to do so and met with disappointment and frustration). Though I have officiated at numerous rabbinic functions in Israel, with the approval of the rabbinate, I have never presented myself as more than a local congregational rabbi.

Probably – if we had it to do all over again – there would be no official rabbinate here in Israel, and more people would have a greater affinity to Jewish tradition. Yet the official rabbinate does perform vital functions in Israeli life, and it's hard to imagine how *kashrut* regulation and other religious institutions would operate without it. That said, I'm reminded of the old Jewish aphorism said in truthful jest: "The world is full of all sorts of people, and I'm glad I'm not one of them."

Living in Israel is not without its emotional challenges. The fact that our children all live in America was and is difficult for me – and it was especially difficult for my wife. On the other hand, one of the greatest benefits of living in Jerusalem was that we could really know and treasure our grown grandchildren who came to study in the Land of Israel after high school. They were regular Shabbat guests and often brought their friends along.

For some years, while my father was still alive and well, my wife and I accompanied him to a hotel in Tiberias for Pesach. One or two of our younger grandchildren from the United States always came with us. One grandson, a notoriously finicky eater, was once with us for Pesach. On *erev Pesach*, we arrived at the hotel in time for a "light lunch." There is no such thing at Pesach hotels: A tremendous spread of all types of food was on the buffet table. Our grandson toured the buffet, then informed us that there was "nothing to eat." I never actually enjoyed a hotel stay over Pesach. Even when we were allowed a "private" *Seder* (with about ten other people), I was uncomfortable. When my father could no longer make the trip to the hotel, we adjusted, and he celebrated Pesach at his seniors' residence. He instructed us to go be with our children in America for the holiday, something we gladly but regretfully did for quite a few years.

Just living in the Jewish state is exciting and gives meaning to even the most mundane tasks and happenings. I'm reminded of an incident related by Rabbi Eliyahu Kitov. He was walking in Jerusalem with a Jew visiting from America. His guest was full of criticism regarding Israeli society. Rabbi Kitov interrupted his tirade, saying, "Why waste time discussing these negative topics? Let's take four large steps and walk on! That's doing something positive, for the Talmud promises great reward simply for walking four ells in the Land of Israel."

I walk a lot in Jerusalem, and as I do, I think of Rabbi Kitov's wisdom. Success generally depends upon the right perspective. Living in Israel certainly provides that.

Chapter 12

A Global Approach to Teaching Torah and History

"The Destiny Foundation has become my personal destiny as well."

When I decided to leave Shaarei Torah and move to Israel, I felt it was time for me to undertake educational projects serving the larger Jewish world. The broad circulation of my tapes and the popularity of my lectures had convinced me that Jews around the globe would be interested in viewing, and supporting, such efforts. So I created the Destiny Foundation, based then in a very small office in Monsey. I was very fortunate to find a most talented, industrious, creative, and loyal administrative director, Elaine Gilbert. All the income from my recorded lectures now went to support Destiny.

In Jerusalem, another skillful and devoted person, Miriam Cubac (in fact, her whole family), headed the foundation's Israeli projects. My friend Rabbi Danny Tropper, founder and head of Gesher (an organization that promotes mutual understanding between religious and secular Jews in Israel), allowed us to use a small office in his organization's building in Jerusalem. We've since moved to the city's Ramot section. In Israel, Destiny regularly sponsors tours, *Shabbatonim*, and lectures, and distributes all our products. It also creates lecture series and organizes an annual banquet in Jerusalem as well as book launches and premieres of our movies.

The American office organizes lecture tours, book events, movie premieres, and annual summer tours to many interesting and exotic places around the world. My weekly *parshah* sheets and articles on Jewish history and current events are now posted on websites created by our American office: RabbiWein.com, Jewishdestiny.com, and Jewishhistory.org.

For almost twenty years, the Destiny Foundation has been a major supplier of curricula, materials, information, and guidance to more than three hundred and fifty Jewish schools worldwide. Its reach has become vast: It has had an effect on many Jews, and on the world Jewish scene.

I'd long had an idea of producing films that would make Jewish history come alive for Jews and non-Jews of all ages and backgrounds. (Of course, with today's technology, they are videos and DVDs, but in my mind they're still "films.") My first project was a biography of Rashi, the great and immortal eleventh-century French commentator on the Bible and Talmud, whom I have loved since I was a child. I knew nothing about producing movies, except that I had to find someone who knew *everything* about it – and to find a great deal of money to finance this venture.

In the late 1980s, I spoke in Atlanta at a banquet for the local day school. Afterward, visiting some dear friends, I shared my movie idea. They told me that their neighbor's brother, Ashley Lazarus, was an award-winning film director and producer from South Africa, then living in New York City. The neighbor, Beverly Beard, very kindly gave me all the contact information for her brother, and upon my return to New York, I got in touch with him. He was enthusiastic about doing a film on Rashi, and we agreed on a critical point: Rather than having a live actor portray Rashi (which to me bordered on sacrilege), the film would be animated.

So now that I had the movie expert, I just needed the money. A decent, hour-long animated video would cost approximately $1.3 million. At that point, Destiny had about $100,000 in the bank. When Jackie and I were in Switzerland one summer, I met a noted philanthropist who wasn't that interested in contributing to my yeshiva, but he donated $75,000 toward the film. Even then, I didn't have enough even to begin.

And then I experienced something that occasionally happened to me in my years of raising money for Torah causes: a moment of serendipity.

Every year, I made a short fundraising trip to Miami Beach on behalf of Shaarei Torah. I always visited a very wonderful local resident, Leon Sragowicz, who was unfailingly kind and solicitous to me, though his donation to the yeshiva was relatively modest. That year, as I was leaving with his usual donation in my pocket, he stopped me at the door and asked if I was working on anything else to spread Torah. (He was a big fan of my taped lectures and distributed them widely to his circle of friends. In fact, he helped place them in JCCs and even in prisons nationwide.) I told him about my idea for a film about Rashi, which would reach tens of thousands of Jews in a different and unusual manner – at least as far as the Jewish synagogue/school world was concerned. He invited me back into the house, and we sat down to discuss the project. He gave me $500,000. Later, Ashley Lazarus, Elaine Gilbert, and I visited with him, and he gave us another $250,000. All in all, I now had $1 million in hand, and we embarked on making the movie.

Rashi: A Light After the Dark Ages was produced at Disk-In Studios in Tel Aviv, and I visited often during work on the film. What a fascinating collection of talented and creative people! Since we know nothing about Rashi's appearance, the artists used their imaginations. He ended up a composite of photographs of many great Eastern European rabbis. The animators worked diligently from those photos, trying to capture the "look" of a great rabbinic leader. Among the staff were a number of new immigrants from Russia, whose artistic skills were truly amazing. One project leader told me he'd researched his family tree and was convinced he was descended from Rashi; he felt privileged to work on a film about his illustrious ancestor.

Ashley Lazarus turned out to be the cinematic genius he was touted to be. Talent, patience, and vision are his stock-in-trade. The film was a great success and has been viewed by tens of thousands of people. It is part of the Jewish history curriculum in hundreds of schools worldwide.

Rashi was followed by another animation, *Rambam:The Story of Maimonides*. This production, too, was very well received throughout the Jewish world. Premieres for these films were held in many cities in America, Israel, the United Kingdom, and South Africa. I attended most of these screenings, addressing the audience on Destiny, Torah, and filmmaking.

Most people who worked on these videos were secular Jews with little previous knowledge of the subject matter. Suddenly exposed to a Jewish world they knew little about, they were dismayed by their ignorance of their own heritage. Through these projects, many were deeply influenced and came closer to the understanding and practice of Jewish tradition. That alone justified the effort and cost of the films.

The financial strain was such that the Destiny Foundation took a hiatus of a few years before embarking on new projects. We had borrowed money to finish the Rambam video, and that money had to be repaid. We also owed Ashley and the production people, and I hate owing anyone. It's hard to interest donors in a film project, especially after the film has already been completed. Also, few people are willing to contribute toward debt reduction. Nevertheless, Destiny somehow paid off all the debts incurred in the production of these two major films as well as a shorter one, *Of Heaven and Earth*, based on Hasidic tales.

Anyone raising money for Jewish causes knows he needs the help of Heaven. I make no claims for my holiness or merit, but I am deeply aware of the unexpected help that Heaven has extended to me and my varied projects over my lifetime. The more than $4 million raised for our film projects testifies to this fact once more. (Unbounded thanks and appreciation go to my beloved friends the Greens, of Zurich and Jerusalem, for their constant consideration, kindness, and support. They are really special people.)

The Destiny Foundation next embarked upon other educational projects, such as a YouTube channel featuring almost one hundred short videos on Jewish history and thought. At this writing, the site has had over a million hits. Destiny also undertook an ambitious project, *Faith & Fate* (based on my book of that name), a series of major documentaries detailing Jewish life and history in the twentieth century, decade by decade. It prepared teachers' guides in conjunction with the films, and this material is used in schools throughout the Jewish world.

The new realm of technology and communication "on demand" has opened up enormous opportunities for the spread of Torah and Jewish values. It has also presented the religious Jewish world and its rabbinic leaders and educators with major challenges. How to deal with texting, tweeting, Facebook, Internet, iPhones, and iPads?! Bans won't solve the problem; they'll be ignored, either blatantly or surreptitiously. There's already a tremendous amount of Torah content available in cyberspace. We should increase its availability and encourage Jews to visit Jewish sites and be involved in Torah wherever they are. Fulfilling the commandment to study Torah in all times and places is well within reach in our generation thanks to these omnipresent new tools. Destiny is working on courses and apps for those interested in Jewish history and thought. This is probably the future of Torah dissemination in this century. We cannot afford to ignore our emerging, technologically sophisticated society; we cannot deny it the echo of Sinai that makes life worthwhile.

There is no rest, but I'm glad. Judaism's attitude toward retirement and inactivity is summed up a Jewish aphorism: "There'll be plenty of time to be at leisure in the next world." The Destiny Foundation has become my personal destiny as well. So I have never "retired" – Destiny's projects, together with my responsibilities as a synagogue rabbi, have certainly filled my days and years over the past two decades. As much as I have sustained the Destiny Foundation, it has done more to sustain me in the latter stages of my life. It has provided me with opportunities, travel, and the means to teach Torah to tens of thousands of people. Unfortunately, it has also forced me to continue in my lifelong role as a fundraiser; but as the rabbis so succinctly put it, "According to the effort and difficulties are the rewards."

Chapter 13

Tragedies ... and Rebuilding

"Resilience and rebuilding are unique Jewish characteristics,
both nationally and personally."

N o one passes through life without tragedy and heartbreak. In fact, the longer one lives, the more susceptible they become. Such is mortality.

My father-in-law, Rabbi Leizer Levin, remarked to me in his last year of life that he had "sat *shiva*" seven times, mourning his parents, two daughters, and three siblings. In the Eastern Europe of his day, this amount of mourning was not unusual. Death was an omnipresent fact of life.

My father lived a very long life. He was over one hundred years old when he passed away peacefully in a hospital bed, being treated for pneumonia. I had been with my father for more than seventy years. When one is with a person for so long, he irrationally believes his loved one will always be there. When my father was buried next to my mother on the Mount of Olives, I found it hard to adjust to his absence. It had been over thirty years since my mother's passing, and I hadn't actually observed a full *shiva* then, since her death and burial were on *erev Pesach*. So this was the first time I observed a full week of mourning. I spoke at length about my father to the hundreds of people who came to visit me, and I found it a great help – a catharsis, if you will, that allowed me to deal with my loss and sadness. Many friends, both old and new, came to console me that week, and it was a very emotional time. My father had outlived his entire generation by many years; therefore my recollections about him and his life were particularly necessary both for me and for my visitors. Condolence calls often turn into banal events peppered by chitchat that has little to do with the life and accomplishments of the deceased. I was determined not to let that happen to my father's memory, so I made it a point to focus the *shiva* conversations.[1]

My father had repeatedly requested no eulogies at his funeral. After consulting with rabbis of note, I didn't exactly follow his instructions. I personally delivered no eulogy at the funeral, which took place in the Jerusalem synagogue in which I served as rabbi, and which he had attended. However, at the end of the thirty-day mourning period, I held a large memorial service in the synagogue, and there I had the opportunity to eulogize my father properly. Though I found odd comfort in arranging for the monument over his grave and in eulogizing him, I always felt he was still with me. What a wonderful person he was! What a wonderful father I had – and still have! My father now has many great-great-grandchildren who bear his name. I pray that they also possess his character traits, powerful memory of Torah, and serene personality.

My wife Jackie had been in good health since her bout of Hodgkin's disease over forty years earlier. However, her two older sisters as well as her mother had died of breast cancer, so she went for regular checkups and mammograms. Her 2006 mammogram revealed something suspicious, and the biopsy confirmed that a miniscule tumor had to be removed. After meeting with the surgeon and reviewing all the test results, we got the impression that it would be a relatively minor procedure requiring an overnight hospital stay. And she would very likely need no further treatment. The surgery was successful, and she was scheduled to leave the hospital the next morning. Our daughter Dena (from South Bend, Indiana) had come to Jerusalem to help with

---

1. The *halachah* prescribes that visitors not address the mourner until he speaks first. I have always felt that the idea was to allow the mourner to direct the conversation and concentrate on the serious issues on his mind, and to avoid the often foolish statements made by well-meaning but insensitive guests.

the recovery. But that evening, Jackie developed a pulmonary embolism and passed away, suddenly and peacefully.

The shock was enormous. A large crowd attended her funeral in my synagogue the next day, and many hundreds came to visit with my children and me during the *shiva* period. I flew to Monsey to observe the last days of *shiva* there and stayed with my son and family for Shavuot.

I was totally bereft. We had been married fifty-one years, and I had so relied on her presence and love. Now our apartment was empty and haunted. The rabbis were correct: The death of a woman touches her spouse most deeply of all.

For a short time, my grandson slept in my apartment so I wouldn't be alone at night, but soon I sent him back to his own lodgings. I considered returning to the United States to live near my children. But I knew that was a purely emotional instinct; its implementation wouldn't have benefited me or the family.

So I decided to stick it out on my own, at least for the year, and try to cope emotionally and practically with my loss and loneliness. My rabbinic duties and writing obligations – the latter all basically self-imposed – occupied my days, but the nights were long and empty. I marveled at how my father had lived alone for so many years after my mother's death. I decided that he was made of stronger and holier stuff than I. The passage of time diminished the shock of Jackie's death, but not the ache and loneliness of her absence.

Tragedies are the lot of everyone in this life and must be accepted as part of God's plan for His world and its human creatures. The Lord apparently expects us to be able to deal with these devastating moments in life; otherwise, He wouldn't burden us with them. Tragedy is one of the supreme tests of human existence. Resilience and rebuilding are unique Jewish characteristics, both nationally and personally. One must strive to acquire and strengthen these traits. It comforts me that many of my beautiful descendants bear their great-grandmother's name. As with my father, I pray that along with her name they inherit her wisdom, grace, modesty, piety, and personality.

Jewish law and tradition frown upon a person living alone for long periods. About eight months after my wife's passing, good friends encouraged me to consider marrying again. I was hesitant, but I realized that if I wanted to remain productive and regain a sense of happiness in life, I should remarry. My children agreed that remarriage would be best for me. I was frightened by the realization that this was an enormous undertaking on my part.

Nevertheless, when a dear family friend from Miami Beach recommended a certain woman from Lawrence, New York, I took the plunge. The Lord blessed me with the right woman at the right time. Mira Cohen and I met, courted, and married. She left her children in America, moved to Jerusalem, and took on the public role of *rebbitzen* with graceful aplomb. She has proven to be everything I could have hoped for – a loving wife and a great *rebbitzen*. Her family and mine have meshed into one, and I am daily grateful to her for rebuilding my life and strengthening me in all my endeavors. The stability she has

Mira and me (Ayer's Rock, Australia, 2013)

brought to my home and life has enabled me to keep up with my writing, lecturing, counseling, producing videos, and being a synagogue rabbi. I can never repay her for her sacrifice and devotion. The Lord has showered me with many blessings throughout my life, and Mira is certainly one of the major ones.

My father was a very private, modest person. He didn't allow publicity about himself, and he influenced me greatly in that regard. I am not my father – certainly not in modesty or piety – but like him, I have studiously avoided self-promotion. This policy has stood me in very good stead as a congregational rabbi in Jerusalem. Allow me to employ an analogy from the wilds of Africa: When I toured Africa on safari, I noticed that we rode in open jeeps and Land Rovers that pulled up very close to the leopards, cheetahs, elephants, hippos, rhinos, and even lions. I wondered why the animals seemed to ignore the vehicles and their occupants. The guide explained that the animals don't view a vehicle as a threat: It has never harmed any of them, and it blends easily into the scenery. In their eyes, our jeep was just part of the landscape. This imagery is a good metaphor for the rabbinic situation here in Israel. I have alluded to this in a previous chapter, but it bears repetition. When rabbis new to Israel advertise their lectures, their Israeli colleagues feel threatened. Certain American rabbis suffered considerably from criticism by the Israeli rabbinic establishment. If one keeps a low profile and blends into the rabbinic landscape, he isn't perceived as a threat and can truly enjoy substantial freedom and accomplish much. So I never advertised my Shabbat Shuva or Shabbat Hagadol lectures. As mentioned, I also eschewed recognizable rabbinic garb in Israel: The moment one dons the big, black hat and long, black frock, the danger of being viewed as a threat increases exponentially. My years here in Jerusalem have taught me that very valuable lesson.

I feel very flattered that many younger rabbis ask me to help them solve congregational problems or prepare sermons and lectures, or just to listen to them pour out their frustrations. I receive these calls almost weekly from all over Israel and the Diaspora. I attribute this phenomenon to a Talmudic adage: "If perhaps wisdom cannot be found here, at least age and experience can."

Much of this traffic was sparked by my book *Tending the Vineyard*, which is really a primer on the realities, problems, and opportunities of Jewish public life. My students stay in touch with me as well, and I have made many new friends in the rabbinic world. I treasure their friendship and confidence in me.

Yeshiva students regularly seek my help in charting their course in rabbinics and/or Jewish education. No two people are alike, so I offer no one-size-fits-all answers. Overall, however, the problems of young men entering the field of Torah service are terribly similar. Usually the most I can do is lend them a sympathetic ear and let them freely express their trepidations. I remind them of an apt anecdote told about Rabbi Yisrael Lipkin of Salant. He wished to send his devoted disciple Rabbi Yitzchak Blazer (Peterburger) to St. Petersburg to serve as the rabbi in that capital of the Russian Empire in the nineteenth century. The city was known to be highly cosmopolitan, and the Jews there quite assimilated. "I'm afraid to accept the position," Rabbi Yitzchak confessed. "What will happen to my piety?" Rabbi Yisrael responded, "Whom, then, shall I send? Someone who *isn't* afraid?"

Jewish public life entails great risks, personal and moral. Only risk-takers should enter the field.

Living in Jerusalem has generally brought to me a sense of serenity regarding my life and the future of the Jewish People and its nation-state – even during the wars and intifadas. I am certain that Diaspora Jews are always more concerned about developments here in Israel than are the Israelis themselves. The Talmud attributes a "churning, angry, and frustrated heart" to Babylonian Jewry – i.e., Jews living in the Diaspora.

Of course, I've given up certain activities because of my advancing years. Realizing and acting upon one's limitations is much better done earlier than later. The main change in my lifestyle is that I no longer drive in Israel. For various social, economic, and psychological reasons, driving in Israel is – as mentioned – very challenging even under the best circumstances. So for me, taxis have become the preferred mode of transportation. Sitting in the backseat of a taxi gives one a different perspective on life, especially when the trip is enhanced by the sagacious observations of Israeli taxi drivers.

Even with the crazy traffic and unsettling news events, the most placid period of my life has been my time here in Jerusalem. This is one of my most striking feelings regarding my move to Israel. Jerusalem has added years and quality to my life, and I am eternally grateful to God for the opportunity to live here.

Chapter 14

Hopes and Blessings

*"Surely I have lived through one of the great historic
chapters of the Jewish story."*

By definition, an autobiography has no final chapter. I hope
and pray for many more years of health and productivity. But when one
reaches a respectable old age, as I have, one is more than satisfied to take
life one day at a time. Very long-range plans seem unrealistic.

Yet the Talmud tells of an old man who planted trees that would
bear fruit only seventy years later. When asked why, he replied, "My
ancestors planted for me; so too do I plant for succeeding generations."
So a much longer view is necessary, stretching beyond our own lives.

For millennia, intergenerational human communication was possible only through the written word. But today, through the miracles of
technology – with sound and sight as lifelike as can be – one can reach
many unborn generations. Posterity remains the true judge of the influence and value of one's life and works.

History always has the final say on people and events. Many
times a person unrecognized in his lifetime is elevated by later generations to a place of prominence. Conversely, many a contemporary hero
is judged by subsequent generations in a more harsh and critical light.
As Maimonides wrote regarding the furor and criticism heaped upon
him regarding certain of his works, "We must wait fifty or sixty years till
all of those who act out of jealousy and malice are no longer alive – and

then the books will be judged upon their merit and worthiness solely, and so they will then either rise or fall." Judaism teaches that even those who have passed on are judged not only by their life's achievements and failures, but in the light of their effect on later generations. Therefore, any judgments regarding a person's life are certainly premature. And if judgment is made by the person himself, it is certainly biased.

I have high hopes for my grandchildren and their descendants. They are pious, talented, and – most important – committed to the survival and success of the Jewish People and to the study and dissemination of Torah knowledge and values. Through them and their accomplishments, grandparents live beyond the grave. The achievements of later generations justify the efforts and investment of previous ones.

A strong sense of family is an important value in Torah life. Family requires tolerance and precludes narcissism. I have often mentioned that family feuds are the bitterest of all. No family escapes unscathed, for every clan includes different personalities and outlooks, giving rise to resentment and hurt. Nevertheless, my fondest hope is that our family remain whole, cordial, cooperative, and free of strife, pettiness, and jealousy. In that sense, grandparents are a uniting focal point in fam-

Me with my granddaughter Leah Ziskind and her four children

ily life. This is perhaps the greatest contribution they can make to their descendants' well-being.

In my lifetime, I have seen the Jewish People at its lowest point, immediately after the Second World War and the Holocaust. Had someone told me then that I would someday be a rabbi in Jerusalem, the capital of a Jewish state – and live to see the miracles that the existence and strength of that state represents – I would have been very skeptical. But never doubt the fulfillment of the eternal Jewish dream.

Dancing with my great-grandsons
at a family wedding

Surely I have lived through one of the great historic chapters of the Jewish story of the ages. I appreciate this special gift that the Lord has granted me, and the goodness of life He has bestowed upon me. There is ample reason to believe that the Lord who has seen us through this far will see us to our complete redemption as well.

Upon reading a portion from the Torah scroll in the Temple in Jerusalem on Yom Kippur, the high priest of Israel would announce, "More than what I have read to you is written herein." The same is true of this book and my life. But what's written here will suffice. Not everything need be recorded. All blessings to you for sharing my life story by reading this book. Now consider writing your own story. Your descendants will appreciate it.

The fonts used in this book are from the Arno family